Note:

Since this book was published, VA forms
and form numbers in Appendix C have changed.

Please check with your local Veteran
Services Representative to determine the correct
forms and form numbers.

The telephone number and address of your local
Veterans Services Center is available on the internet
or in a telephone book.

The current address and telephone number for the
Santa Clara County Veterans Service Center is:

June 2015 (could change in the future)
Office of Veterans Services
68 North Winchester Blvd.
Santa Clara, CA 95050

Making Peace With Military Post-Traumatic Stress

Getting Help and Taking Charge of Your Healing

DOUG NELSON

BALBOA.
PRESS

A DIVISION OF HAY HOUSE

Balboa Press books may be ordered through booksellers or by contacting:
Balboa Press
A Division of Hay House
1663 Liberty Drive
Bloomington, IN 47403
www.balboapress.com
1-(877) 407-4847

Because of the dynamic nature of the Internet, any web addresses or
links contained in this book may have changed since publication and
may no longer be valid. The views expressed in this work are solely those
of the author and do not necessarily reflect the views of the publisher,
and the publisher hereby disclaims any responsibility for them.

The author of this book does not dispense medical advice or prescribe the use
of any technique as a form of treatment for physical, emotional, or medical
problems without the advice of a physician, either directly or indirectly. The
intent of the author is only to offer information of a general nature to help you
in your quest for emotional and spiritual well-being. In the event you use any
of the information in this book for yourself, which is your constitutional right,
the author and the publisher assume no responsibility for your actions.

Any people depicted in stock imagery provided by Thinkstock are models,
and such images are being used for illustrative purposes only.
Certain stock imagery © Thinkstock.

Printed in the United States of America.

ISBN: 978-1-4525-8131-6 (sc)
ISBN: 978-1-4525-8132-3 (e)

Library of Congress Control Number: 2013915728

Balboa Press rev. date: 11/04/2013

Table of Contents

Dedication vii

Chapter 1   Prologue—To a Soldier 1

Chapter 2   Being a Soldier—A Historical Perspective ... 5

Chapter 3   Post-Traumatic Stress 11

Chapter 4   Healing from Post-Traumatic Stress 21

Chapter 5   Making Peace with Those Who Love Us .. 41

Chapter 6   Making Peace With Ourselves 51

Chapter 7   Making Peace with the Dead 57

Chapter 8   Making Peace with the VA 63

Chapter 9   When We Don't Treat Each
              Other As Brothers and Sisters.................... 85

Chapter 10   Bad Discharge 93

Chapter 11   Citizen Soldier 99

Chapter 12   Conclusion 117

Appendix A   Resources 125

Appendix B   Books that Have Helped Me 129

Appendix C   Sample VA Forms 21-0781 (stressor
              statement) 131

Appendix D   Agent Orange.. 145

Glossary 151

Dedication

My heartfelt gratitude goes out to the US Department of Veterans Affairs Health Care System and Vet Center professionals who have given so wholeheartedly and unselfishly of their time, talent and expertise to help me and so many other veterans.

I must acknowledge the thousands of veterans of all our nation's wars, who, wounded in body and in spirit, carry themselves with dignity and who live decent, caring lives. My father, Kenneth D. Nelson, Jr., a WWII combat veteran, showed me how to live with post-traumatic stress. He loved our mother and their four children. He did his best for all of us.

I wish to acknowledge especially the late Peter N. Linnerooth, Ph.D. He was there for me and for so many others in his US Army and Department of Veterans Affairs careers. Pete is greatly missed.

CHAPTER 1

Prologue—To a Soldier

I saw you in the airport, in desert-pattern combat fatigues, a duffle bag over your shoulder. Briefly, I saw myself in 1968, in this same airport, my head nearly shaved, my uniform looking like a clown suit on my skinny frame, on my way to Vietnam.

You were surrounded by people, either not noticing you, not wanting to disturb you, or, in this urban America way, not wanting to appear un-cool by speaking to a stranger. No one ever spoke to me, either. Other veterans and I have spoken to some of you, though, to tell you to take care of yourselves and each other over there, or, if your boots were dusty and you looked tired, a "Welcome Home."

I am touched and humbled by your willingness to serve, as our protectors and as our ready armed forces. Many of you flocked to enlist when our country was attacked, because you believed that you would be going after the very people who attacked us. Perhaps yours was a purer motive than mine. I enlisted because I had dropped out of college and was faced with the draft. My chosen path was, in those days, one of least resistance. You and I freely chose to be soldiers. We make the best of our situation, try to survive it, and try to get our buddies though it unharmed.

This book is for you, a soldier, sailor, Marine, Airman or Coast Guardsman serving in the active military, Reserve or Guard. It is also for anyone who has served or is contemplating military service. "Soldier" is a catch-all term I use for the sake of convenience. By "soldier" I mean any and all of you.

I served in the US Army for four years, one in Vietnam and two in Japan. I am no war hero. I was a scared skinny kid. In the light of protecting my buddies, it made more sense to do my job than not to do it. I did my signal intelligence job so that an enemy transmitter would not escape detection, and so that perhaps the infantry soldiers flying out every day on air assaults would not chance upon an enemy unit they did not know was out there. After college on the GI Bill, I worked for six years in the US Veterans Administration as a contact representative, and as a technical writer for the Department of Defense for nearly twenty years.

I worked as a veterans services representative for local government before I retired recently. I did Department of Veterans Affairs claims work for those of you who have health and mental issues from military service. I continue to assist veterans on a volunteer basis.

I am struck by the ambivalent feeling many of us have about our service. We want to believe someone is better off because of what we did when we were under arms wearing our country's uniform. We are proud that we went where our country asked us to go and did what our country asked us to do. Yet there seems no end to wars, as we see still another generation on foreign soil, fighting to take care of themselves and their buddies, fighting to live another day and to get the Freedom Bird home.

I am also troubled by America's view of us. It is as ambivalent, I think, as our own. All the detective dramas in the 1970s featured episodes about the veteran gone berserk. The lip service of yellow ribbons and praise is somehow different when we come home looking for jobs, when we re-enter college, and when we seek out the benefits promised us for our service. We find ourselves back in the airport.

Had someone discussed war with me in these terms, it might or might not have made some difference in my life. My dad came close when he tried to talk me out of enlisting for the Vietnam conflict. I had to see it for myself before understanding what he was trying to tell me.

I meet and speak with so many of you that I am forced to sort out my own feelings about my war, your war, war in general, and about the universal experience of the soldier. The experience of going to war was so profound in shaping my views of the world, of my country and of war in general that I am still trying to make sense of it. This book, then, is the product of my thoughts and feelings. It is short enough so that reading it will take only a little of your time, but it covers the things I have been carrying around with me for four decades.

I focus on post-traumatic stress (PTS) because it is the inevitable result of sending people off to war. I was a non-combat soldier who had three very bad days. I struggle with PTS. I am humbled by those of you who were in combat, facing booby traps, IEDs and enemy fire of all kinds nearly every day you were in country. You may have served more than one combat tour of duty during your enlistment. Your PTS may be more severe than my own. You may have been wounded. The work you may need to do to take charge of your healing process will require much of your inner resources. Please know that you are not alone in your struggle, and people in the VA system are ready and willing to give you help with post-traumatic stress. The struggle is worth the effort because you are worth the effort. Your spouse and children are worth the effort.

Many veterans, my father among them, cannot talk about their PTS, combat fatigue, whatever their generation's term for it is. I am willing to talk about PTS, for you, as part of my own self-therapy, and for our fellow citizens who sent us to war.

CHAPTER 2

Being a Soldier— A Historical Perspective

You and I both grew up believing that it is the duty of Americans, particularly men, to serve our country in the military. There is an underlying message that we are to define ourselves as men in this light. My great-great and great-grandfathers were Confederates, both grandfathers were in WWI, my father was in WWII. My son served seven years in the army, and was medically discharged with a disability. I wore my father's Combat Infantryman Badge on my Davy Crockett T-shirt, and proudly wore the GI helmet liner my father brought me from the army surplus store.

Perhaps, like me and my peers in Vietnam, you have found it a matter of practicality to accept the ethos of the warrior, because it is necessary for your survival in a hostile environment. You are justifiably proud of your competence and skills. The professionals who trained you in the arts of war, for their years and experience, are even more skilled than you, so you follow and respect them. Perhaps you are a professional soldier and choose to remain so.

For the soldier, it is your war, justified because you are in it. It is not your job to make foreign policy; it is your job to carry it out. If you relay radio messages, prepare meals for hundreds, or walk combat patrol, you do your job so that your buddy can do his. Your buddy is the most important person in your life; you do what you can for him, and you depend on him for your very life. When you cannot keep him from harm, you grieve.

Ours is the brotherhood (and sisterhood) of the soldier, a part of the universal human experience. The American soldier is still only a soldier, serving under arms to further what others have judged to be in the best interests of his country. If we read history, we should know that we share this experience with Israelites and Philistines, Roman legions, Moors, Napoleon's divisions, and the men of every European and Asian nation having armies. No leaders have ever lacked men willing to fight, suffer and die for them—not Genghis Khan, George Washington, Lincoln, Hitler, or Bin Laden. They all manage to convince us that we are meant to be part of a grand effort, of something far larger than ourselves, our families and our village. They may appeal to fear, or revenge for some wrong committed against you, or these motives may give way to hate, pure and simple.

Every soldier thinks that his cause is unique in human history, his devotion to that cause most justified, most righteous, most pure. Your enemy is the one trying to conquer the world, to annihilate your people, to destroy your way of life, to enslave others. Our own cause seems without fault, built on unassailable logic and truth. I found a Nazi belt buckle among my father's things. It had, above the Nazi eagle and swastika, the words, "Gott Mit Uns" (God is With Us). Soldiers have been all equally devoted, equally ferocious in battle, equally believing in a righteous God at their side, Crusaders and Arabs alike.

As terribly costly as WWII was, almost no one questioned the righteousness of the war, or its cost. The enemy was clearly attempting mass conquest, genocide, and unspeakable brutality. There was no disagreement on the necessity of bringing their depredations to an end.

Your war and mine involved occupying another country, under arms, in places where much of the population perceives themselves as being occupied by an oppressor nation. We are caught between our feeling that, as our government told us, we are "bringing democracy" to that country, and what we had to do in order to, in our view, keep order, determine who our enemies are, and deter those who would attack us. We share the experience of being under arms in a country where we are not welcome. The most cursory reading of military history makes clear the tremendous risk of forcing an opponent to defend his own home territory. We can expect the men and women of that country to fight us hard and to fight us smart. If another power were to attempt to occupy the continental United States, we would be hanging their blackened bodies from the nearest bridge. I suppose they would term us something like "insurgents."

The yellow ribbon you see on the backs of cars these days says "Support the Troops." The word "troops" has no legitimate singular form. Political leaders and generals like to think in terms of troops. They cannot dwell on the individual suffering and death that war entails. "Troops" implies a faceless, nameless mass, to be moved like chess pieces, instead of as individuals, each life precious. I see implicit in the word a wish for the horrors of war to be left to military professionals and to the willing soldiers, like us, so that the accountants, firefighters, teachers and brickmasons among us don't have to deal with it. We don't like to be reminded of the heat, danger and horrors you face every day. Like me in Vietnam, you are "other people's kids," troops, kept at a distance in the airport, when you come home wounded, and when you come home looking for a job.

I doubt that the French treated Napoleon's returning soldiers, or the British treated those from the Crimean War, any better. The combat experience is so far removed from what the working stiff in our country experiences, that they don't know what to do with us, or what to say to us. Aside from celebratory victory parades, such as those in Washington, D.C. after the Civil War, they cannot relate to what we have been through, where we've been or what we've done.

For Vietnam veterans, the yellow ribbon is a declaration that, regardless of how we feel about the justification for the war, we will not allow you to be denigrated, ignored, and abused, as we were during and after Vietnam. When that war became unpopular, we became unpopular. We veterans know that war is not the fault of the warrior upon whose shoulders we place it.

Why can I not accept the fact that war is an inevitable consequence of the human condition? Since our society, like every other one in history, is able to convince some of its members to fight and die while the rest of us go on about our business, why not let soldiers do what soldiers do, and assume victory or some vague semblance of it?

I am not at ease with our eagerness to use military force. When I see you going house to house in places like Fallujah and Baghdad on the evening news, my stomach churns, and my wife sees that I am uneasy. Bringing force to bear against the specific people who attacked us makes sense, if only to ensure that it does not happen again. Invading and occupying entire countries makes far less sense.

We sowed the seeds of this reluctance to resort to war as an instrument of national policy ourselves. We have created weapons so terrible, so unthinkably devastating, that we assume no one would dare to use them. We forgot an inevitable consequence of military technology—that whatever we have, someone else will copy, steal, buy or figure out for himself. We could not prevent the old Soviet Union, Israel, India, Pakistan or North Korea from obtaining nuclear weapons. We have not been successful even in preventing the proliferation of high-capacity, rapid-fire weapons among children in our own country.

I think that diplomacy, intelligence-gathering, and international cooperation have become more essential, not less. We simply have to learn to get along with the rest of the world, accept less than we'd like to, give more than expected, and act as a more mature, more intelligent, more compassionate and wiser nation.

I will have more to say about what I think the role of the soldier and veterans might be in forcing our fellow citizens to consider the effects and consequences of war.

CHAPTER 3

Post-Traumatic Stress

The only real experts on post-traumatic stress (PTS), aside from those trained people whose job it is to treat it, are those who have it. I have it. I can talk about it, I can objectify it, and I can try to explain it to people for whom explanation is necessary.

This condition has, for years, been known in the definitive Diagnostic and Statistical Manual in all its Roman-numbered editions as Post-Traumatic Stress Disorder. I agree with some in the treatment field that the term "disorder" may tag a person who has it with an unnecessary stigma. People who have it can be said to be struggling with or suffering from post-traumatic stress. The "disorder" of post-traumatic stress results when it affects our personal relationships, our ability to study or to earn a living, and our peace of mind.

Post-traumatic stress (PTS) is not a personality disorder, not the low end of bipolar disorder. PTS is not, as some sheltered armchair commentators have suggested, because soldiers don't love their country or God enough. PTS is not a weakness, or anything lacking in the ethos of the warrior.

PTS is outrage on a deep, profound level. It is not to be trivialized as political outrage or anger at the enemy, even when they killed and maimed your buddies.

Let me tell you about outrage. I had the poor judgment, when my son was about 2 ½, to let him sit with me on the sofa while we watched a barroom brawl on TV. He began crying, and I asked him what was the matter. He said, "They're breaking up the furniture." When you're this small, you don't go out much. Your world is the furniture. No one broke up furniture at his house. He was outraged.

Here is where the analogy ends. In combat, or in situations in which your life and safety are threatened and you feel helpless, it is not STUFF that is being broken. It is everything you have learned from your mom and dad, from church, from school about who we are in relation to other humans, about how we humans are to treat each other, and about what we can expect from others around us. What is broken is what you think you can expect from the rest of your life.

PTS is a sane person's reaction to the insanity of combat and to the effects of war. "Post-traumatic" means after the fact. Vietnam veterans are still coming to terms with PTS forty years after they were in combat. From my claims work the past five years with people struggling with and in treatment for PTS, I believe we are among the most sane of people, that we are less, not more, likely to commit acts of violence. We have seen and experienced the violent and the insane. We are, generally, among the last to want to inflict violence on others. Very few of us take up hunting.

PTS can have its cause in a particular traumatic event, or it can stem from prolonged threats to life, such as combat. Personal assault often brings on PTS. The trauma of having been wounded or assaulted affects one's sense of safety and security. The prolonged fear of trauma or of a repeat of a past trauma can bring on PTS.

We relive the event or events in some way. Some describe it as a tape that plays over and over again. Some of us see the event as we drop off to sleep or in our dreams. I know an Iraq veteran who, in a more literal sense, plays back the video he shot from his truck, and looks for the wires he thinks he should have seen before the truck in front of him was hit by an IED. For some of us, it is not the actual event, but the situation in which it occurred. The truck driver who was constantly in fear of an attack on his convoy, and the base camp soldier exposed to repeated mortar and rocket attacks are frequent examples I encountered in my work. Many veterans have nightmares of being sent back to Vietnam; in the case of Iraq and Afghanistan, they may actually have experienced the nightmare of being sent back.

Most of us are "triggered" by sights, sounds, even smells. A hole in the ground reminds me of the hole our captain helped us dig before he was killed. Thumping sounds remind us of incoming rounds of enemy fire. Fireworks, or the smell of gunpowder, are common triggers for guys who were in infantry combat. Some of us cannot stand the smell of meat being broiled for reasons too terrible to relate.

We have trouble sleeping. Events or situations visit us in the night, when it's quiet. We can drop off to sleep but awaken intermittently, or at some particular time. For me, it is 3AM. Some of us are easily startled by sudden noises, even such things as a dropped dish at home. We were conditioned by combat or by the dangerous situation to be on the alert, to be prepared if we have to fight off an attack, or to take cover from incoming fire.

A level of awareness, of hypervigilance, is necessary for combat, something people who have not been through this cannot imagine. A soldier feels he cannot be vigilant enough, cannot pay too much attention to his surroundings. One slip-up, one second of inattention, could mean the death of his buddy or himself. You must see the trip wire, the place where the ground just doesn't look right, the sniper on top of a building.

Years later, the world is not a safe place any more— not your home, not your car. You were so intensely unsafe, or for so long a time, that you have lost the concept of safety. I know guys who prowl the house at night to be sure no one is trying to get in. I know of guys who take a driver cutting in front of them in traffic as a personal threat to their safety. I hiked the

Appalachian Trail with a combat veteran who pointed out possible ambush sites and likely enemy bunker locations.

Every soldier knows it could be he who is killed or wounded tomorrow, or on the next mission, or one day before he is to go home. This is especially tough on folks who have been in prolonged or frequent combat. There is no end in sight; the missions go on, the laying of ambushes, the patrols, the firefights. Unlike those of us who were in Vietnam, young people are now serving multiple combat tours.

It is because of the profoundly violent nature of what we experienced that we have a tendency to expect disaster, confrontation, or a shortened life. I cannot stand to watch the crime stories on TV that my wife watches. She wants to see justice done; I do not need the reminder that the world is violent, and often unjust.

A reaction to what we experienced is to numb ourselves, so that we will not be hurt or triggered again. What we tend to numb ourselves against is both ends of the emotional spectrum, the funny, and the joyful, as well as the hurtful. I think that my Dad, a WWII combat veteran, struggled with PTS. I learned from him to keep a lid on it. What we also keep a lid on is friendships with other men. Much of the time I would rather be alone, with work or hobbies that keep me busy. I don't want to be hurt again when I lose friends. A hiking buddy who was lost and died of exposure, veteran clients who died before their claims could be processed, and the loss of friends of my dad's generation take me back to the loss of my captain in Viet Nam.

In my old age, and after treatment for PTS, I find myself hypersensitive, after many years of numbness. It is not only to the sights and stories of soldiers and Marines in Afghanistan and Iraq, but to violence of all kinds. I find I cannot tolerate television at all. The preponderance of violence seems to trivialize it, and also to give violence a legitimacy that, because of its relatively rare actual occurrence, it does not deserve. I am hypersensitive to injustice, especially when people suffer because of capricious, legally sanctioned injustice.

A common characteristic of PTS is misdirected anger. As we know, anger in us men is often displaced. It is often generalized, and is not about the incident at hand at all. We cannot explain to others what the real problem is because they would not understand. They haven't been there; they haven't done that. They have not been in such a situation of helplessness that they have felt totally impotent, with no way to prevent a disaster or to provide help after the incident. We have probably heard that depression is anger turned inward. We know that turning our hurt onto others, even onto those we love, is not helpful, and may drive people away who otherwise love us and care about us.

Some of us miss the adrenaline rush. A friend went to bars to get on the wrong end of a conversation, so that he could get into fights. He looked into house windows at night, not because it mattered what people were doing inside, but because there was a considerable element of risk. Some want to be police officers, because they miss the comradery and the danger element of combat.

I have heard recent war veterans say that they wish they were back in Iraq with their buddies. As terrible as war is, how you and your buddies react to the situation is predictable. You know you can depend on your buddy and he knows you've got his back. There can be comfort in the known, terrible though it may be. In the field, you knew things would be done right. We lose patience with co-workers and others who can't follow directions or procedure, or have no concept of known strategies with predictable outcomes. We tend to be very judgmental about obviously irresponsible behavior on the part of others, from such small things as throwing trash on the street to serious issues, such as texting while driving. We wish we could impose order in the situation. As young soldiers, we railed against strict military discipline and order, and find that, later in life, we miss that order and predictability.

Back home, it might seem no one can be trusted, not your co-workers, not people in authority, such as the police, and at times not even the people who love you. We avoid crowds, such as at Wal-Mart, arts and crafts shows or even the grocery store. Our trust is broken, on a profoundly deep level. We tend to back off from other people, to isolate ourselves. We expect hostility or confrontation, even when we have no clear indication that we will be threatened in any way. We don't want to deal with how we might explode at someone, so we isolate ourselves to be sure that this does not happen.

An all too common way to deal with PTS is to self-medicate with alcohol or drugs. Do this while in the military and you risk a less-than-honorable discharge and loss of education benefits. We compound our problems, having addiction to deal with as well as PTS. Addiction is a sure way to bring on the disorder in PTSD.

Allow me to dispel a myth about "combat fatigue", "shell-shock," or if you will, PTS. It has absolutely nothing to do with the perceived righteousness of the war, whether on the part of the veteran or on the part of his society. I meet people who cannot stand the sight of Jane Fonda, and just as many who joined war protests as soon as they came home. We still have veterans of the ultimate righteous war, WWII, suffering with PTS. All these decades, they haven't known where the anger, the alienation from other people, the nightmares were coming from.

Unlike WWII veterans, veterans of Vietnam and of the Middle East wars tend to lose their faith in government, and even in their countrymen. Vietnam veterans felt abandoned, unwanted, sneaked into the back door of the country in the dark of night. Many of us had a particularly tumultuous relationship with the Veterans Administration that made us cynical and untrusting. Middle East veterans may feel that no one cares that they serve multiple combat tours, some in both Iraq and Afghanistan during one enlistment.

Combat and fear for your life are not the only causes of PTS. Women (and men) who are sexually assaulted have PTS. This happens frequently enough in the military that I devote Chapter 9 to it. We see it in women in the military who were treated not as sisters in arms but as objects to be exploited and abused. We also see PTS in young people who, by accident of birth, grow up in an atmosphere of violence and fear. Our former (and present) enemies have PTS. A Vietnamese who experienced B-52 strikes struggles with PTS. In this sense, we are brothers and sisters.

I have attempted to explain some common symptoms of PTS, for those of us who have been exposed to incidents and experiences typical of those that result in PTS, for those of us who have loved ones who may be suffering, and for those of us who, whether policy-makers or voters, place people in situations that are likely to have this result.

I believe that healing from post-traumatic stress is possible, even if no magic pill or words can cure it.

Healing is possible to the extent that we understand the nature of the beast that followed us home from the war, and recognize that we must deal with it every day. Healing is a process of dealing with post-traumatic stress every day so that it does not become a disorder for that day.

Your Vet Center or VA Mental Health Clinic will help you to begin this healing process. Let the day you walk through the Vet Center or VA clinic door be the first day of your healing process.

CHAPTER 4

Healing from Post-Traumatic Stress

Before you read further, do this:

Sit in a comfortable chair, feet flat on the floor. Breathe in deeply, so that your abdomen pokes out. (If yours is like mine, it pokes out, anyway.) Then suck in a little more air. Now, let it out slowly, taking at least as long as you did breathing in. If you are standing, let your knees bend slightly; don't lock your knees. Let your tongue rest at the roof of your mouth.

Do several of these deep breaths. Do this before you fall asleep. Do this in traffic. Do this in the waiting room of the Vet Center. Do this whenever you feel anxious, especially when there doesn't seem to be any particular reason for being anxious. Be in the moment; be mindful of bird calls, the wind, and of your own breathing and heartbeat. This helps me, and I think it might help you.

All of us who struggle with PTS need the help of trained professionals for guidance. The VA is the best place to get this guidance. I can only tell you that I believe, from the point of view of one veteran who struggles with PTS and is going through his own healing process, that the VA's structured treatment approach to PTS will help you.

One purpose of writing this book is to encourage you to seek help from these unselfish, giving people. They will guide you in your healing process. I think that you can heal from PTS, just as you can from any other wound. PTS is a wound to the spirit. Like a bullet wound to the leg, there will always be some scar tissue, some tenderness, an entrance wound and an exit wound. You will come to know what makes the pain worse, and how to deal with it. Like with a wounded leg, healing is a process, not an event.

You will probably not wake up some bright and sunny morning completely cured of PTS. The doctor can't give you a magic pill, and your counselor has no magic words. Money from the VA does not cure post-traumatic stress.

I believe that the severity of PTS is directly proportional to the intensity and duration of combat. The symptoms I have discussed may be more severe in the veteran of heavy, prolonged combat. Veterans who have combat wounds or personal assaults to deal with are more likely to have severe PTSD. Dr. Jonathan Shay talks about the worst kinds of PTSD in his twin books

Achilles in Vietnam and Odysseus in America. He calls the PTSD from prolonged combat and accompanying wounds complex PTSD. His work is especially valuable to veterans who have had the responsibility of leadership. If, as he says, PTSD is the undoing of character, then in our treatment and our self-therapy, we need to be concerned about the restoration of our character.

A second purpose of this book, besides encouraging you to seek help, is to help you to see the need for taking charge of your own healing, to embark on an arduous journey of self-therapy and growth.

Dr. Jill Bolte-Taylor is a Harvard brain scientist who suffered a stroke that severely damaged the left hemisphere of her brain. She writes in My Stroke of Insight about the healing that is possible from brain damage, with more clarity and insight than do most of us who have not suffered brain damage. I believe that post-traumatic stress rewired my brain. I think that the source of the "fight-or-flight" reaction, my amygdala, is too easily triggered by my fears, forebodings and emotional reactions to things I perceive to be threats. I recommend you read what she has to say to us about the complementary functions of the left and right sides of our brain. The left side of our brain classifies, categorizes, compares, analyzes and calculates strategies. The left side lets us sequence and properly place events and things in time and space. My left-brain approach to human problems is one that a mechanic would use to diagnose an engine problem. In the right-brain "in-the-moment" mode, things that happen are experienced as they are, without analysis, classification or judgment. The left brain enables me to operate a camera, fiddling with shutter speeds, apertures and sensor sensitivity, but the framing of the scene of redwoods in the fog comes from my innermost feelings, coming intuitively from the right brain. At the present time there is nothing I would rather be doing than writing this book for you. My left brain gives me the tools to write this book and my right brain makes me want to write this for you. Dr. Bolte-Taylor suggests, quite rightly, I think, that I can, and should, train my brain to be aware of its right side, its non-verbal, non-analytical function and to train it to turn aside destructive, violent, or hurtful thoughts. We can pause, breathe deeply and slowly, seeing our harmful habit-pattern, emotion-driven behavior for what it is and dealing with it rationally.

Reading, counseling, and group therapy will help you know the nature of the beast that followed you home from combat. Just what is this that I have, and what do people think who have this, and how do people act who have been through what I have been through? You can read and agree, in your mind, that you have PTS, but still not be able to deal with it emotionally. Like the alcoholic at his AA meeting, you must own the fact that you have PTS. You are not weak, you are not lacking in the "Hooah" ethos. You are not crazy, you have not "lost it." You have PTS because of what happened to you. Your response to this outrage is sane.

Your response to rational adults killing each other and innocent children who get in the way is sane. Own your feelings; they are yours, and because they are yours, they are valid.

I experienced EFT, Emotional Freedom Therapy, at a veterans' conference. The practitioner, who was not a doctor, social worker or therapist, had me sit and relax. She showed me pressure points on my head, elbows and chest, and showed me the sequence of tapping these points with the tips of two fingers. Frankly, I felt silly. When she asked me what happened in Vietnam, she then turned my story into a context for owning and accepting my feelings. I did the tapping sequence— center of forehead, cheekbones, upper gum line, chin, chest while repeating, "These feelings are real, they are mine, I own these feelings, I love these feelings." I cried for Captain Casey, my captain who was killed in a mortar attack; I wept uncontrollably. I had cried for Captain Casey and for Chris (a buddy in my unit) only at the Wall, when I saw their names. Afterward, I felt as if a burden had been lifted. This kind of therapy, or one of its variations, might work for you. Although the VA currently does not consider EFT to be a preferred method of treatment, give it a try, if you have the chance. Your therapist or doctor may use other strategies to help you deal with your emotions.

My EFT experience was a structured way of putting me in the moment, in a state of mindfulness. The emotion is here and now, it is valid—embrace it, deal with it. Thich Nhat Hanh offers excellent discussions of mindfulness and on dealing with anger in more than one of his books. Mindfulness or being in the moment is cultivated in Asian martial arts, tai chi, yoga, transcendental meditation and other forms of mental discipline.

We men who have been raised in the West have heard from childhood, "Suck it up, don't be a baby, crying is for sissies." We are brought up to stuff our feelings, to roll them up and put them on the top closet shelf of our minds. When we do that, our hurt comes out as anger, and we turn this hurt onto others and onto ourselves. Our outrage at what happened to us, our hurt and our confusion slide downhill on lubricated skids of anger and we react, and overreact, driven by pure emotion. The books I have referenced about PTS and about anger make it clear that we need to own the anger, embrace it, recognize it and deal with it. Recognize that it exists, that your hurt is being manifested as anger, and take responsibility for the damage it might cause, both to you and to others. Our feelings about lost buddies, combat trauma and about war itself are valid; our misdirected global anger needs to be controlled. We can control it, by redirecting, retraining, or reprogramming our brain.

In <u>An Operator's Manual for Combat PTSD, Essays for Coping</u>, Ashley Hart sees the right brain as the source of harmful emotional overreaction. What science knows about the brain is mainly theoretical. No dissected brain has ever been found to be labeled as to parts and functions. Based on my own understanding, I prefer Dr. Bolte-Taylor's theory of brain function, but anyone discussing brain function as it relates to PTSD would agree that our brains are amazingly malleable and resilient. We can change our ways of thinking, regardless of what part of the brain we think we are using to do this.

I try to make time for sessions of deep breathing, thinking only about the rhythm of my breaths, or the cadence of my steps and being totally aware of what is happening right now, including the fact of my own anger or anxiety. I cool down, letting the cool outside air in and the hot air of anger out. I must first relax. Newer VA therapy methods begin their sessions with structured relaxation. Some counselors teach combining breathing with yoga, Tai Chi or even some martial arts exercises. I am better able to deal with it constructively. Instead of *"My captain is dead, I am angry, I am hurt, how much longer and how much more is this going to suck the joy out of my life?"* the moment becomes *"Yes I am angry. I feel the anger, I accept it, I embrace it. There is good reason for my anger, but I am in control. I am going to breathe, relax and give my powers of reason a chance to help guide me as to how I should act, instead of reacting out of emotion."* If you are practicing Tai Chi or another movement discipline, your breathing, relaxation and movement exercises will have some benefit for you. Do not impose pressure on yourself to learn the entire Tai Chi sequence unless you have good reason yourself for learning that.

Practice mindfulness in situations that have nothing to do with PTS-triggering events or sensory stimuli. I was very surprised at the effect of this practice when my wife and I took a simple walk on the beach in the morning. I asked myself, *"What are you feeling right now?"* It occurred to me to tell her, right then, "There is no place in the world I would rather be right now, and there is no one else in the world I would want to be with." This is pure in-the-moment right-brain activity, distinct from the analytical left-brain side. This kind of experience is purely intuitive. In this magical short instant, the Pacific Ocean, the salt air, the sunshine, and my love for her became one. My eyes tear up when I think of it.

I have been offered EMDR (Eye Movement Desensitization and Reprocessing) treatment. It involves dealing directly and vividly with the traumatic event(s), and with your bodily and emotional reactions, using a method of controlling eye movement. I intend to try this therapy, and will let my readers know if it helps me. Try it yourself if the VA offers it to you. I am finding that VA treatment professionals will offer some course of treatment, but never mention it again. If you are interested in or want to try EMDR, Emotional Freedom Therapy, yoga, Tai Chi or any other treatment your therapist mentions, you might remind him/her of your interest.

Recently, VA has been offering trained companion dogs as therapy. They can be trained to sense anxiety levels and to discreetly place themselves between the veteran and others in crowd situations. Caring for the dog is still another level of therapy.

Your doctor has the authority to prescribe medication if he thinks you might benefit from it. I have taken medication to help me sleep and to help me to deal with anxiety. Be sure to express to your doctor any concerns you have about the strength of the medication, drug dependency, withdrawal issues and side effects.

The doctor or the Vet Center counselor will help and guide you, but it is up to you to do the work of healing. It is work. It requires listening, thought and a lot of self-examination. It involves being in a group with other vets who are struggling with you. Whether you are with a Vet Center counselor, a doctor, or in a group therapy, be there fully (mentally as well as physically), speak the truth, and put any thought of results out of your mind. What you are doing has nothing to do with your VA compensation claim. You are there to heal.

You will learn what triggers your PTS symptoms, what makes you immediately angry, what sets off "fight or flight," and what prompts the intensely emotional response that leads to your heart racing, your heart pumping and that solar-plexus, in-the-gut anxiety response.

You will also learn ways to deal with the triggers. The alternatives to immediate emotionally driven reaction involve rational thought processes. Deep breathing may slow you down enough to work on these thoughts. You will hear these strategies in vets' and anger management groups. Be in the moment, be mindful. What is happening right now? I am anxious right now. I recognize it and want to deal with it. The deaths of my captain and of my buddy are in the past; it is not what is happening right now. Collapse the triggering event, let the wind blow out of it. Let it fall into its true importance, let it assume its correct proportion. Street violence and home invasions are occasional problems in the urban area where I live. I wake up formulating strategies for dealing with it if it happens to me, and I am anxious. I slow down, do deep breathing, a few Tai Chi moves and let my reasoning do its job. Is the threat real right now or perceived? Is my perception correct, or is it driven by anxiety and fear? Can I collapse this fight-or-flight reaction, letting the awareness of potential problems keep my wife and me reasonably safe, but not fearful? The unmuffled motorcycle that scared the hell out of me when the guy gunned it in traffic is just that—some boy's toy. Reframe the event; the guy meant no aggression toward me; he's a dumb kid. Reframing often means putting a larger frame around the event. In the larger context of this moment, being temporarily startled is not so important, not so disruptive to my life. Finally, let it go. Don't hold onto it. One rationale used by one of my therapists for potential road rage incidents is, "I don't have time to be his therapist." More constructive responses can become a habit, in that you are reprogramming the way your brain responds to startling events. You may still have the sharp, emotional response to triggers, but you can develop the habit of collapsing, reframing and letting the emotional reaction go, because the true situation does not call for reaction.

I am in my healing process. I was not told the VA would help with this until my recent work with veterans. I did claims work with the VA twenty-five years ago, in Virginia. The only claims I did for PTSD were on the psychiatric ward. I had no training in it. Since I was not a patient on a psychiatric ward, I assumed I did not have PTS. I denied I had PTS for forty years. It was only after talking with hundreds of veterans in the past six years that I realized my symptoms were the same as theirs.

My healing process began when I decided to go to a Vet Center to open up about what I had been dealing with. This particular Vet Center did not have an orientation. I sat down for an hour every week or two with a woman trained in counseling. I came to trust her, and looked forward to these meetings. I could lay events and feeling on her I would not have laid on my wife. She peeled away my childhood, my adolescence and my failed marriages to show me that PTS does not occur in a vacuum; one aspect of my life cannot be viewed in isolation from the rest of my life.

The "disorder" in "post-traumatic stress disorder" is in the ways we turn this mental anguish on ourselves and on those who love us. We have to be led to see that we are doing this. We have to be led to see that self-destructive behavior, such as drug/alcohol abuse, is not working for us but against us. A good PTS counselor doesn't preach to you, doesn't give you words to live by. By listening carefully to what you are saying and by asking the right questions, he/she will lead you to reach certain conclusions.

A year later, a counselor who was a combat veteran led me, through skillful questioning, to reach a needed conclusion, that "I have to stop wallowing in this shit." I need to take charge of my own healing and to do the work necessary to break old habits of reacting and thinking. In my addiction to angry thought and angry speech, I was no better than any other veteran with poorly controlled PTSD.

I do not consider myself to be healed. I am in a process, in a struggle. I am better than I was, but PTS is still part of who I am. The struggle is with myself. I can revert to old, unhelpful ways of reacting to people and events around me, or I can use the tools I have been given to deal with the emotions that surface from time to time. I can still become inappropriately angry, or react to an event as if I need to be in "fight-or-flight" mode, even when the situation does not call for it.

When we do overreact, speaking or acting inappropriately, we tend to be hard on ourselves. We care what other people think of us. We can't beat ourselves up over these lapses. All of us backslide, on all fronts. Let those who care about you know what's up and move on. Handling anger, dealing with stresses in your life, treating those close to you the way you really want to treat them—all these are part of a process. Dr. Phil's pop psychology contribution to people who struggle with PTS is "Own it, take responsibility for it."

When you try to deal with PTS, you may feel at first as if the symptoms are getting worse. Please understand that nothing can be any worse than holding on to this as you have been doing. It DOES help to talk about what you are feeling. Talk to your treatment professional and to those you will meet in group treatment.

The most recent development in my treatment has been group therapy. I meet every two weeks with nine other Vietnam veterans. Like me, they have made mistakes in life, and are dealing with their emotional state. If I did not revert to alcohol or drugs to self-medicate, it is through some undeserved grace; I am not better than someone who has had drinking and drug problems. I am just more fortunate in this respect. My addiction is to anger. These nine vets are the sanest people I know. It does me good to be with them. Each of us "checks in," telling what has happened in the past weeks, how we reacted appropriately or inappropriately to triggering events or to personal conflicts. We share with each other the progress of our VA claims. The facilitator is a veteran with PTSD. He interjects certain healing principles into the conversation. I find his remarks repetitive—in fact, reassuringly so. The current example of a helpful strategy, in response to one of our problems, might hit home in a profoundly personal way. Among ten veterans, each guy's experience will shed light on my own situation.

Vet Center-sponsored groups eventually disband. The resources are not available to keep groups going forever. Many groups, however, decide to continue meeting, for breakfast, lunch and scheduled meetings. We find that we need each other, and that we can offer support when a buddy needs us. For many of us, the group keeps us from going back to isolating ourselves.

Not all group therapy is VA-sponsored. Vets4Vets was started by a Vietnam vet, but is made up of Gulf War, Iraq and Afghanistan combat veterans. When I tried to sit in on one of their meetings, I was told, "This is only for vets of these wars, Mr. Nelson." I tell my young veterans that Vets4Vets is veterans only, no geezers, no shrinks. They share experiences and offer support.

Not every self-healing strategy that we veterans come up with on our own is inappropriate. My dad, many other vets I know, and I all need to keep busy. We keep busy until we are tired, so that we sleep better. We keep busy to feel useful, to do something that has results that we can see. Other people may not see our business as productive; my house when I was a kid had the neatest lawn and the cleanest car on the block. My Dad had to be busy. An Iraq veteran I know is restoring an old farm house, and learning construction, wiring, and plumbing skills. Some rebuild and restore old cars or trucks. One of my veteran friends collects and restores old farm tractors.

A self-healing strategy I find helpful is to do what you enjoy doing. Some of my vets fish for the peace and quiet, for being outdoors and to develop their fishing skills. Groups of veterans like motorcycle riding. The Rolling Thunder group makes a yearly pilgrimage to the Wall in Washington, D.C. If you were a musician before military service, don't let the music die. Get out your guitar, get your left-hand calluses back, and revisit those riffs and runs. Listen to the music you love. It is part of who you are. Your music can be a way of getting back in touch with who you are. Some of us have artistic skills, are good at photography or sculpture. Reconnect with things you like to do. Art and music are therapy to such an extent that people make a living as art therapists, working with veterans.

All hobbies involve problem-solving. This is good brain exercise. Why is this engine running rough? Is this an ignition or a fuel delivery problem? How can I improve my golf swing? Why am I getting such a wicked slice on the long drive? Can I depend on automation in my digital photography to handle exposure, focus and color balance, or do I have to take charge of these functions? That's a great riff I'm hearing in that guitar piece. What key is he in; is he running the bass line with his thumb independently of the treble? How does he do that? Have fun doing what you do. You enjoy doing this because you are good at it. You look forward to doing this, and you get up in the morning either anticipating doing your thing or looking forward to the time you can do it. It is one area of your life that you can control.

Try to adopt an attitude of openness to new places, things, books, thought and people. Pay attention to what other people do for fun.

Try to transfer this positive attitude over to other areas of your thoughts. I can control how I react to things in life today. I can handle whatever happens; I can do this. Believe me, I struggle with my attitude. I have a hangup about a shortened future because of what happened to three of the guys in my company in 'Nam. I will always be dealing with this, but I am getting better.

Be thankful you are here on earth. Remember the time the plane landed that brought you home. Be thankful for the health you do have, and for the functioning brain and the powers of reason you possess. Practice naming off what you appreciate about your life. It is a way of reprogramming the harmful thought-patterns that followed us home. It is an ongoing process; it is work.

Some of us find that we can relate only to other veterans. We have no patience with non-veterans who want to hear "combat porn" about things they cannot begin to comprehend. When we meet another vet, we do not necessarily tell war stories, but we have an immediate rapport. This may lead to attending unit reunions or trying to reconnect with buddies. In the last years of my Dad's life, he tracked down buddies. The one he really wanted to find had been running a peanut farm only 35 miles down the road in southern Virginia. It was an attempt on his part to find meaning in his WWII service, to revisit where he had been and what he had done. He and Mom went out with the vet and his wife several times.

All religious and spiritual traditions have important things to say about suffering. To be sure, PTS is an intense form of suffering. Read, listen and weigh carefully what is being said. The relevance of the message depends on who is speaking, on his/her experience, and on particular institutional filters through which a message must pass. I would separate myself from any church that preaches intolerance, self-righteousness and hate, whether it is directed toward gay people, the less fortunate, other religions or some political opposition. Perhaps irreverently I refer to the three largest religious traditions (Christianity, Judaism and Islam) as "sandbox monotheism," because of their common place of origin. Their mutual antagonism is one of the greatest of human tragedies, because their teachings are so similar. All three offer profound truths about acceptance, forgiveness, unconditional love and introspection. The Christian tradition in which I was raised helps me to deal with anger and self-righteousness. I have found relevant and practical guidance in Buddhist teaching, because it emphasizes practice over doctrine.

The single best act of self-healing is to find someone else who needs your help. This is great therapy for the self-imposed isolation many of us experience. A plumber who has PTS has taken on a young veteran with PTS as an apprentice. A vet who has struggled with both alcoholism and drug addiction is mentoring a young man who is having addiction problems. Many volunteer opportunities exist, at parks, historical sites, and at VA Vet Centers, clinics and hospitals.

Keep in shape, exercise and eat right. Many vets walk or bike for therapy, many for miles at a time, many in parks or wilderness areas. Combine walking, swimming, running, yoga or tai chi with the breathing exercises we talked about. Practice mindfulness by being conscious only of your steps and your breathing and forget your destination or things you have to get done. Hit the gym for the upper-body and weight work. Go to a nutrition class at your VA Clinic. You can learn about the pernicious effects of excess salt, sugar and fat, and also of overeating in your diet.

The American food industry is not interested in our healing. Read up on the effects of excess sugar, in all its insidious forms, and the high salt and fat content of packaged snacks and highly processed foods. With the help of your VA dietician, get in touch with fresh vegetables, fish, and low-fat meats, in reasonable portions. My own diabetes was brought on, in part, by not paying sufficient attention to diet and exercise.

A successful VA claim for PTSD, traumatic brain injury, or for something else you may have suffered from military service will bring you validation, because the country that sent you to fight in the war they wanted finally recognizes that you went, you were in combat, and you are forever affected by how that changed you. In the event the claim is not successful, find out why it was not successful, and find a vet rep to help you to take it to the next step. This claim's outcome is not healing or failure to heal in and of itself. See it as a paperwork exercise that went well or did not go well. Continue to read, listen and work through your healing.

Veterans my age have, according to actuarial statistics, about twenty more years to love those we have said we love, to heal relationships, and to try to be the men and women those we left behind in Korea, Vietnam, Iraq and Afghanistan would want us to be. You younger guys have a lot more time to work on your healing. You have people who care about you, who want to help you and know how to help you. You don't have to wait 40 years.

Please know this. The hundreds of combat veterans with whom I have spoken and for whom I have done claims have taught me something no one else could. Your decent treatment of me, your compassion for my PTS and my Agent-Orange-related diabetes—and, most importantly, your control of your own frustration and justified anger—have shaken me to the core. We are the living; we are the sane. We are more sane than those who sent us to war, and those who sat by silently while they sent us and not their own children. Our reaction to insanity is reasonable; any other reasonable person walking in our boots would react the same. You are my Dad, keeping a lid on it all his life. You are my brother vets who go off fishing or hiking when you need space. You are the vet who volunteers at the VA, still giving. You are the vet having breakfast or lunch with fellow vets, offering fellowship and your help.

It's time, brothers and sisters. Let the healing start now, or let your healing continue.

Welcome Home.

CHAPTER 5

Making Peace with Those Who Love Us

In treatment circles, the word "disorder" is being phased out of "post-traumatic stress disorder (PTSD). I do think, however, that the word aptly describes the effects of uncontrolled PTS on our families. PTS is a disorder when we turn our hurt and our anger onto those who love us as well as onto ourselves.

I think that the healing process is like the Alcoholics Anonymous Twelve-Step program, in that we need to try to make peace with the most important people in our lives—those we've said we wanted to spend the rest of our lives with, and also our children who have been born of the desire of two adults to be together.

We are not the same people who went off to war. When we come back sullen, angry, reactive, and hyperaroused our families are confused. They don't know any more who we are. We scare them; we don't speak and act in ways they expect us to, and we can even drive them away from us. They can then harden their hearts against us so that they avoid us just as we avoid things that trigger us.

We cannot expect them to understand our hypervigilance, our sensitivity to noise and disorder, or our desire to be away from other people at times, including them. While we were serving overseas, our wife (or husband) took on the responsibility for the children, the home, the car and a job. She (or he) may have done things differently from you, but still got them done. We may feel unneeded, having left our spouse in charge. I am home and she is still in charge. The children still see her as the head of the household. Who am I, then?

We have been deeply hurt, and we isolate ourselves in an attempt to keep from being hurt again. Our peace and our expectations about the future, and our perceived role as leader of the family have all been damaged, and we are trying to head off being hurt still again.

In fairness to those we love we must level with them and tell them what we are going through. We have seen terrible things that we would rather not tell them about. Events, scenes, sounds, and even smells can trigger responses that we need to survive in combat. These responses are appropriate in a combat situation, but cause only confusion and misunderstanding once we are home. Level with your spouse about what you experienced and about what you are feeling about your role in the family.

Be sure to get treatment for any of your attempts to self-medicate with alcohol or drugs. Like owning the fact that you have PTS, own the fact that you have an alcohol or drug problem. The VA should be your first source of help.

I saw one veteran's custom-made baseball cap at a VA Clinic that read, "Vietnam Veteran with PTSD, Leave Me Alone." We do not want to define ourselves and, by extension, our families by our PTS, any more than we would want our hospital nurse to define us as the "adenocarcinoma in Room 314." In the same way, we do not want to define ourselves or our families in terms of alcoholism and drug abuse. We can be veterans and families who struggle with PTS and other issues. PTS is our problem, and it may be the family's problem, but it is our business, our struggle. You can count on VA treatment professionals to honor your right to confidentiality and privacy. As an individual, you play roles besides that of veteran or PTS sufferer. You are a husband or wife, a father or mother, a co-worker, a student. As difficult as it often is to deal with PTS, it is not who you are.

Everyone has heard of post-traumatic stress, but fewer people know that it is treatable. Take your wife, husband or significant other to this place where they are helping you with your PTS. He/she will see other veterans like you and the place where you spend so much time away from home, and where you go to get help. Let your life partner know you are continuing to get help. If the VA Mental Health Clinic is part of your treatment, let your partner know that you see a doctor there, and that you might be prescribed medication, to help you sleep, to help with anxiety, or to deal with other symptoms of PTS. Some Vet Centers have classes for spouses, so that they can learn more about what you're dealing with.

Wives have brought their husbands in to the Vet Center or to my veterans services office, and tell me that this is her husband's last opportunity to get help, because she cannot take it any more. I told these veterans, "Do you know why your wife is here with you in my office? She loves you, brother. She loves you enough to be here with you. She wants you to start the healing process for your PTS." It does not matter whether it is the veteran or the spouse who finds out what PTS is and that there is treatment for it. What matters is that they do find out.

You are married to, or are in some other way, committed to this person. At some point in your lives you made a promise, in front of family and friends, to join together with the possibility of creating new little people with him/her.

The marital or parental relationship may be in need of healing. In his <u>Anger, Wisdom for Cooling the Flames</u> Thich Nhat Hanh gives specific wording for when you approach a spouse or child to talk about your anger—or theirs. He advises setting aside a time to talk, and about admitting that anger is a problem, about not blaming the other person, and about trying to discover the "seeds" of anger inside yourself. Bring issues out into the open. Acknowledge them, own them.

I would adapt his dialogue for my own situation this way: *Darling, I am angry. I am not controlling my anger very well, because I am causing pain to the very person I love most in the world, you. I don't think, though, that my anger is your fault. I am doing my best to deal with my problems. I am trying to put into practice the tools the Vet Center gives me, to take deep breaths and to hesitate before saying something to you or the children. I need your help with this. Can you help me?*

Adapt such suggested wording for your own situation. Work together through your issues with your VA Vet Center or clinic professionals.

When you both are ready, seek the help of a trusted counselor or minister to consider renewing your wedding vows, and acknowledging your mutual love and trust in a formal way, in the presence of friends and family. As someone trained in cultural anthropology, I believe in the function and benefit of ritual. All of us understand the value of the wedding ceremony, Holy Communion, and funeral services. Military or hospital chaplains might want to look at the possibility of a ritual of re-bonding for families affected by PTS, once they have committed to therapy.

Two factors can stand in the way of familial healing. One is violence, directed at a spouse or at children. In that case, the spouse, usually the wife, has to separate from the veteran for her own safety. Few would argue with her need for safety and security. If your spouse and children need to separate from you to protect themselves from physical violence, you must get help for this, or else accept the loss of your family. They have the right to safety and security.

A second factor can be a third party to whom one of the spouses is directing affection and attention. Often this third party offers security and emotional support a veteran suffering from PTS cannot give. But it can also be the veteran himself/herself who is seeking attention and affection elsewhere. In the face of serious marital problems, the other man or woman will always look better. We must either seek professional counseling to mend this or resolve to deal constructively with the consequences.

In dealing with the breakup of a marriage, resolve to stay in touch with your child or children and remain in their lives. Then be sure to do this no matter what. Children need both their mom and their dad.

Of the choices we make in life, none is so profoundly life-changing as choosing to love. We all know of times in our lives when we have chosen not to love, for practical reasons or even in error. To choose to love is to choose to accept who this person is, this person's behavior, past and present, this person's physical presence, his/her habits and ingrained opinions, and this person's reactions to what you say and do.

Give some thought and effort to making everything you say and do reflect your choice to love him/her. Our words and actions are our choice to love made real.

As is the case when dealing with PTS, you will make mistakes, you will say and do things that do not reflect love. Own it, take responsibility for it and talk to your loved one.

I had to renew the decision I made to love my third wife. I reached the point in my healing process where I needed to reconfirm my love for her. I claim no special wisdom here; I just had a gut feeling that this needed to be done. I am thankful for having her in my life. I will try to live my life so that what I do and say is a direct reflection of my decision to love her. Although I think she is an easy person to love, I will still always have to stay focused. Such manifestations of love can be as simple as assuming some duty the spouse dislikes, even something as trivial as washing the pots and pans, or driving hilly, curvy mountain roads. After all, she buys and cooks the food, and she drives in cities.

To enter into an adult relationship in the first place, or to reconfirm a relationship, is to be vulnerable, to lay ourselves open. This means allowing another person to see us at our best and at our worst, and everything between the two extremes. Yet we may tend to think it means setting ourselves up for more pain when the relationship doesn't work out, and sometimes we would rather not put ourselves at risk for more hurt.

It's true: we are in fact putting ourselves at risk when we open ourselves to loving a partner. We are either willing to accept that degree of risk, or we are not. Weigh the options, look honestly at what you can or cannot accept about that other person, and decide whether you want to commit your life to this woman or man.

Children are the result of a man and a woman choosing to be together. They are suddenly in our lives, screaming and helpless. They are not always cuddly and lovable. Early on, however, your daughter melts your heart with her little toothless smile, or your son comes to you with his baseball glove and wants to play catch. You love them when they are easy to love. Making the decision to love them, without any conditions involved, even when they are not so lovable, is what parents do. Covering your buddy and carrying out your mission is what soldiers do. Your buddies depended on you to be there for them. When you have children, your mission is to raise them to be responsible loving adults. They do not have the life experience to make decisions about what is good for them. You have the experience and knowledge; you walk point for them. You continue to love them when they throw a wild party at your house when you're out of town, or when they wreck the car. You will see them walk across the stage to get a high school diploma or college degree; you will see them make the choice to love someone else and walk down the aisle.

If you are lucky, the commitment and the decision to love and honor your spouse will be the same as the commitment to love and raise the children the two of you brought into the world together. If your marital circumstances are different, stepchildren deserve no less from you. You are an important adult in their lives; in loving their parent, you have chosen to love them.

My hope for young veterans is that each of you will experience the joys of committed love and of children born of that love. I hope to see you in the park, a little one riding up on daddy's (or mommy's) shoulders, your spouse or partner beside you. Visualize yourself as a committed, loving, fully functioning dad, mom or partner. Keep this vision in your mind.

CHAPTER 6

Making Peace With Ourselves

You are home, whether you just got back or you have been home for forty or more years. You know you are not the same person you were before you went to war. People who know you can see the changes in you. People change for various reasons and as a result of their experiences.

You are not crazy. You are the way you are because you lived one of the most intense of human experiences, that of being in danger for your life and witnessing the deaths or injuries of others. You have these feelings because you have a heart in the middle of your chest, instead of a rock. You do not take the deaths of innocent children and of buddies lightly. The fact that these experiences bother you is testament to your sanity, not to any lack of it.

Your deep hurt manifests itself as anger. People around you, including family, might think that you are angry at them. You want to reassure them otherwise, but you also want to shelter them from what you experienced. Like my dad, you would not lay these experiences on them, because you care about them. Our anger is more generalized. Events and situations that hurt you cause you intense pain.

A veteran buddy was sprayed with Mace because he responded too slowly to a traffic cop's order to get out of his car. A young veteran was the subject of a restraining order because of a loud argument with a girlfriend. A Vietnam vet swore he would never return to the VA when he reported mental anguish at a VA hospital in 1972 and was told to "stand over there with the crazies." An older veteran had his PTSD diagnosis brought into a child custody case, which, in part, resulted in curtailed dad time with his pre-teen daughter. Relationships, for whatever reason, go wrong. One person just decides he/she does not want to consider continuing the relationship.

Anger and hurt are often quite justified. To be rejected is one of life's greatest hurts, whether or not we struggle with PTS. In the face of deep hurt, it is difficult to judge how much our PTS has to do with it. Sometimes our pain is so intense that it scares the hell out of us. Sometimes we feel it so intensely that we are sure that our pain is so unique to us that no one else has felt such pain, and that no one else could possibly understand what we are going through. Like some serious illness earlier in our lives, we cannot imagine an end to it. We have been sick for so long that we cannot remember being well.

You may feel a depth of despair that causes you to want to isolate yourself and to lose interest in hobbies, relationships, work and studies. As one who struggles with PTS I can tell you that it is not unusual to have these feelings. Well-meaning friends, counselors and doctors will tell you about such things as breathing exercises, strange foreign meditation practices, and mental exercises in "mindfulness", "re-framing" experiences and other such seeming psycho-babble that you are sure will not work for you. It has worked for other people, perhaps, but you are convinced none of it will work for you. Your pain is too great.

We men have a built-in pride mechanism that works against us in situations like this. We don't want to admit that we are hurting, that we cannot handle the situation ourselves, that we are not in control. To admit such difficulty is to admit weakness. We might think that officers, NCO's or Marines don't have these issues. Combat veterans can handle it; they've handled a lot worse. Please know that no one is immune to PTS.

For whatever reason—you were in prolonged combat, multiple combat tours, or a particularly traumatic incident, or perhaps something in your experience and psychological makeup makes this especially hard on you—PTS is, in your case, PTSD. The disorder has kicked in.

It makes no sense not to get help when you are hurting this badly, just as not treating a broken leg makes no sense. As a veteran, your VA Vet Center, VA

Clinic or VA Medical Center are there for you. You need something more than breathing exercises, tai chi or talk therapy. You must be willing to tell the truth to your Vet Center counselor, VA doctor, local vet rep or social worker. All these people care deeply about you and your family. If they did not, they would be keeping accounts, writing software code or teaching children. You are the reason they do this tough, demanding job. If they ask whether you are contemplating taking your own life, level with them.

VA doctors will recommend medication and/or a VA live-in treatment facility if they think you will benefit from such treatment. Let your concerns about medication be known up front. You may tell them that you are afraid of dependence, that you are afraid of long-term effects, or that you don't want to be locked up in a mental ward. A VA residential treatment facility is not a "mental ward." It is a structured, more intense program of treatment that requires that you live on site and interact with treatment professionals and, very importantly, with other veterans.

Veterans came to my veterans services office at the end of their rope, in despair. The former Navy corpsman, after forty years, couldn't take any more. The infantryman from Iraq and Afghanistan said he'd had enough. I immediately sent them to the nearest VA clinic, and called ahead to tell the clinic to expect them. In the several such cases I saw, this was never the wrong thing to do. I am not a therapist and have no training in psychology. I sent veterans to people who do have such training and experience.

A veteran friend committed suicide. He had relationship problems, as do many people. At the same time, he had difficulties on the job, as do many of us. He, in an instant, opted for the most permanent of "solutions" to his temporary problems. He left his friends, his parents, his young children and his veteran clients with intense, lasting pain. Additionally, he left them without his caring, his decency and his dedication. All of us who loved and respected him remain shaken to the core. Any one of us who knew him would have spoken with him and listened to him.

Please, brother, sister, take care of yourself. Go to the right people and ask them for help. These caring people have no idea you are out there unless you go to them. Your brother and sister veterans care more about you than you will ever know. They have your back the same way they did in Iraq or Vietnam.

If you have a loved one with these issues, take him/her to get help. If it seems they are not being helped, intervene on their behalf. Another Vet Center counselor, another Vet Center or another doctor might, for some reason, be a better match for your veteran.

We put these young people into harm's way, we asked them to go where we sent them and to do what they did. Whether it was forty years ago or five years ago, they need our concern, they need our help.

CHAPTER 7

Making Peace with the Dead

Before we go to war, most of us encounter death. As children, we wrestled with the mystery of where Grandpa went after we saw him in his casket. In war, even when we expect to see and experience death, it always blindsides us. It is not the fact that others die, but it is the way they die. This is not a war movie in which our enemies fall like bowling pins, or our wounded merely bounce up as if on hidden trampolines. This is not the painting at Versailles in which the dashing young cavalry officer has a dime-sized spot of blood on this chest, and his comrades anxiously hover over him. Where a living, breathing, laughing buddy stood by us or rode in the armored vehicle, there is a jumble of mangled limbs, crushed head and puddles of blood and soft tissue.

My captain was killed in March 1968 in a mortar attack. He had helped build the bunker that saved my life. When I was introduced to him, I saw a tall, blond crewcut guy a little older than I at the bottom of a hole shoveling out dirt. "I'm Captain Casey. I won't have you do anything I wouldn't do myself. And if you see me doing it, you will be doing it, too."

I was the unit's resident dumb kid. I was sent out to refuel the generators one night. In the dark, I put motor oil in the gas tank. When the inevitable happened, the sergeants were yelling at me, and Captain Casey walked in. "I've been out there. You can't see your hand in front of your face. Why don't we put luminous tape around the gas can, agree among ourselves that it's the gas can, and let Nelson get back to his job."

I did not thank Captain Casey for his help. He was killed a day or so later.

The night he was killed, the enemy was "walking" in mortar rounds, closer and closer. I heard him yell for everyone to take cover. A round hit very close by. It was like a million things breaking—glass, metal pots, wood, everything.

I was sent out for an ambulance while the mortar rounds were still coming in. I didn't know what an ambulance looked like. When I got back, he had been taken away, and I was told he was dead. I was yelled at for staring at pieces of him on the ground.

In May, a fellow soldier, Christopher, was killed coming back to our unit on a convoy. A military convoy is an expedient, usually safe way to travel in country. This convoy came under fire and he was ordered to get down off the truck and return fire. He stepped on a mine. Chris's close buddy was sent to identify his body.

I had first met Chris shortly before we had a beer blast party. We gathered a quantity of beer and had gotten a parachute from the trash dump to shelter us from the sun. Just before the event, it was my turn to wash pots and pans. Chris, a nondescript, skinny, towheaded kid who befriended stray dogs, came by, saw me sitting cross-legged on the ground scrubbing, and pitched in to help me finish. Days later, I was told he'd been killed. I was writing to a sweet girl in Oregon at the time. Her nearly weekly letters were perfumed and signed, "Love, Toot" (her nickname). After I heard about Chris, I burned her letters along with the classified trash. I don't know why I did that, unless it was the thought that I would be the next one killed, and my relationship with this girl was none of anyone's business. After that, I did not burn any more of her letters, and I never told her I burned any.

We didn't handle either loss well. No sergeant or officer talked with us individually or in groups. Each of us was left to deal with it individually. We did have a perfunctory military memorial service weeks later with a chaplain, and the customary rifle with bayonet stuck in the ground and helmet placed on the butt of the rifle.

These incidents resulted in my PTS, although there were others. I put Captain Casey and Christopher out of my mind until I went to the dedication of the Vietnam Veterans' Memorial Wall in Washington, D.C., in November of 1982. I wept when I saw their names inscribed on the Wall. It was the first time I could cry for them, thirteen years later.

I think that the lucky ones can cry. Many of us are too numb to cry.

On the news, I see Iraqis and Afghans weeping openly at the death of a family member in battle, or in some random attack. I think that is a much more honest reaction than sucking it up and trying to macho the pain away. The grief is being experienced together, instead of leaving each person to deal with it alone.

I have heard of military units of company or smaller size having a ritualized way of saying goodbye to a dead comrade. A ritual is a structured way of acknowledgment. People participating in a ritual know the reason for the event and know what to expect. For example, everyone may be given the chance to speak a word of remembrance and there may be some mutual touch—hugs, standing in a circle shoulder to shoulder. Exactly what form this ritual takes is less important than the fact that everyone who knew the soldier experiences his loss as a part of a military unit whose members all depended on each other, had each other's backs, and who loved each other as brothers.

We look for meaning in any death. Our relative or friend lived a long, productive life and it was time to go, or the person suffered and death ended that pain and suffering. We struggle with any death caused by senseless violence or accident, and we must confront painful questions as to whether death in war is any more meaningful than death in gang violence.

I sat briefly at the grave of a young man from my home state at the American Cemetery at Normandy, France. I wondered if anyone else had ever sat with him. I sat with this one soldier, because I could not get my head around over 9,000 buried in just this one cemetery, and 3,000 buried across the way at one German cemetery. We find meaning in WWII combat death in Europe in the context of the sacrifice made to save the world from Nazi depredations. The fact that the German dead did not want to be where they were any more than our own dead is doubly tragic.

If I find meaning in the deaths of Captain Casey and Christopher, it is in their living for their buddies. An exquisitely appropriate line in the song "Touch a Name on the Wall," by Joel Mabus, reads, "This brother here didn't die for no country, he died for me." Captain Casey showed me how to take care of my fellow man. Christopher showed me how to be unselfish. They both lived compassionate lives. I have no choice but to be like them. It is how I honor their memory.

The last time I saw their names on the Wall, before I left the East Coast, I told them goodbye, as I would not visit the Wall again. Little did I know that Captain Casey and Christopher would be riding in the back seat of my mind, all the way out to California. They are with me still, when I need a reminder to take care of my fellow man, and to be compassionate.

Do you need to make peace with someone you lost? Are there so many that it seems like too formidable a job? Did you lose someone you never really knew, because perhaps he was the new kid, and all of you kept your distance because, after losing others, you could not allow closeness again? Were you his squad leader or his commander, and you felt responsible for him? Were you a medic or doctor, saving all you could, but some were just too badly hurt? Do you feel guilty that he had to die, instead of you?

Ask yourself how that person or those comrades would want you to remember them. Do you dwell on their broken bodies, or do you remember how they looked whole, cracking a joke, eating field rations, helping you make a field shelter? Some, if not all of them, will forever be a part of you. You may be alive today because of something one or more of them did.

How do you think they or he would want you to live your life? Would they want you sitting around your house in a haze, or being productive, earning a living, taking care of those who love you or doing something you really enjoy doing?

If you need to adjust something in your life, do it in his name because it is what he would want you to do. If you have been too long not taking care of yourself, please know that he would forgive you, so that you can forgive yourself.

He would want you to give yourself permission to begin the healing process.

CHAPTER 8

Making Peace with the VA

When you come home, you must make contact with the US Department of Veterans Affairs (the VA, from its original name, Veterans Administration). Your first contact with the VA will be the beginning of your healing process. Unless you have independent health care resources most do not, you turn first to the VA for your health care and for help with PTS. You will be dealing with at least two distinct VA functions. You will approach the VA Health Care System for treatment for PTS and for any other disability you may have incurred. Simultaneously, you will deal with the VA disability claim function, administered by the VA Regional Office for your area, to file your claim for disability compensation money. Younger veterans additionally will apply for education benefits under the GI Bill.

For veterans of the recent wars, Vietnam and all other previous wars, the "post-traumatic" in PTS means after the fact, even if it is forty to seventy-five years after the fact. If you think you are suffering from PTS, the following procedures apply as well to you.

VA Medical Center, Clinic or Vet Center, Your First Stop

See your local VA Clinic (or VA Hospital, if that is closer to you) for your health care needs. Within five years of the end of your military service, any health care concern you have is covered. So, this is a good time to get treatment for any disability or injury you might also need to claim later. The sooner after service you get treatment, the sooner it will show up in your VA treatment records. To register with the VA health care system, you need only to put your DD214, copy 4 (the longer copy that shows the character of discharge) across the eligibility desk. If you are a recently returning veteran and you think you have PTSD or traumatic brain injury (TBI), be sure to mention that during your first contact with the VA. The sooner you get help, the easier your recovery might be. At a VA Mental Health Clinic, you will be assigned a social worker who may provide help and who will eventually also assign you to a physician. That doctor can prescribe medication, after talking that alternative over with you. Please show up for all your appointments.

If you are an older veteran who has been told your income is too high for you to be eligible for VA health care, go to your VA Clinic or Vet Center. Show them your DD214, any combat awards you may have, and tell them that you are having difficulty with your war experiences. You should begin receiving treatment for PTSD. Refer to the next section of this chapter for the procedure for filing a VA compensation claim.

An alternative for PTS treatment is the VA Vet Center. These are storefront treatment centers with a small staff of therapists, usually Licensed Clinical Social Workers. Whether you are a returning veteran or a veteran of past wars, you will find your Vet Center to be a welcoming, friendly place. The first person at the reception desk is likely to be a veteran. You will be asked to come to an orientation, or you will meet your counselor immediately.

I like the orientation meeting, because at it you will realize two things—you are not alone in having these symptoms and you are not crazy. Each vet around the conference table will be asked to tell who he/she is, and when and where he/she served. You will not be required to spill your guts about traumatic experiences at your orientation. We veterans don't easily sit in the presence of others and admit we have problems. It takes courage to be here.

Whether it is after an orientation or immediately, you will meet your therapist. He or she may or may not be a veteran. You can, however, be sure that these people want to work with veterans. You can trust them to keep what you tell them confidential, and to be interested in your healing. Open up to him or her. Let them walk point on patrol with you or ride shotgun in the HMMWV. You can't shock them; you can't scare them. They have heard it all. Don't hesitate to "tell this shit to some lady." Women are usually excellent PTS therapists. If your therapist thinks you might benefit from medication, he or she may refer you to the Mental Health Clinic. Have a few help sessions with your Vet Center therapist or your doctor, so that they have records of your treatment from which you can file a disability claim.

Claiming VA Disability Compensation

Once your health and PTS care are started, use the VA claims process to file a claim for PTSD and whatever else you need to claim. By US law, you have the right to claim compensation for injuries or illnesses incurred in military service. PTS is an injury recognized by the VA. In VA claims parlance, the term for PTS is "PTSD." Use that term when filing your claim. Compensation means regular monetary payment of an amount deemed by VA regulations to reflect the degree to which the disability makes you unable fully to seek and pursue gainful employment. Your next stop, then, will be a claims representative (vet rep). A VA clinic or hospital may have a VA rep or people with private vets' organizations (American Legion, Veterans of Foreign Wars, Amvets, Disabled American Veterans, Military Order of the Purple Heart, and others). In most localities, however, your vet rep will work for your state or county. Find them in the blue pages of your local phone book under county or state veterans services. Sit down with this person and try to get a feel for their interest in your claim. Some are more "PTSD aware" than others. Talk to other vets about vet reps who have helped them (or failed to help). Word gets around; you will hear of popular vet reps. These people are popular for good reason. Do not be surprised if your local claims office requires you to make an appointment for a future date. Rarely can you get help on a walk-in basis; these offices can be very busy.

Your vet rep will help you to file a disability claim, and advise you of what to expect from the VA after the paperwork is done. You can help this person by getting VA Form 21-526 from the www.va.gov web site. Have the basic and family data filled out when you see the vet rep for the first time. If you have ever filed a VA disability compensation claim before, whether or not it was successful, claim PTSD on the short form 21-526B. If you are still on active duty and about to be discharged, get VA Form 21-526C and send it in with your military treatment records.

All disability forms have a space to cite what injury or illness you are claiming. Simply put PTSD in that space. Where the form asks when the condition began, put the year(s) you served in Iraq, Afghanistan, Vietnam, etc. The place of treatment will be your Vet

Center, VA clinic or hospital, or a private doctor, if that applies.

Whether or not you claim other disabilities besides PTSD depends on how quickly you need the compensation money. Claiming only PTSD gets you quicker action on your claim.

For Veterans With Combat Award(s)

If you have a combat award—Combat Infantryman (or Medic) Badge, Army Combat Action Badge, or Navy or Marine Corps Combat Action Ribbon, Navy Fleet Marine Force Combat Device, Bronze Star with the "V" device, your service's Commendation Medal with a "V" device, Air Medal with "V" device, Silver Star, Congressional Medal of Honor, Distinguished Service Cross, Navy Cross, Distinguished Flying Cross or the Purple Heart—you can do the shortcut VA Form 21-526EZ. The "EZ" form is for claims that need no further development. With evidence of your combat award (usually on your DD214), you will be sent quickly to a VA doctor who will determine the severity of your PTS. You can wait until that claim is completed to claim such problems as hearing loss, tinnitus, joint injuries, or chronic illnesses. You do not need to have a diagnosis of PTSD in your military treatment records or from VA treatment to file a claim for PTSD. Your combat award speaks loudly.

For Veterans Without Combat Award(s)

Veterans claiming PTSD who do not have a combat award (I was one) must fill out VA Form 21-0781 to document that you were in a hostile fire situation. Essential on that form is your unit, the dates you served in a combat zone, and the place(s) you served. If you are a Vietnam vet, the tactical zone (I Corps, III Corps, etc.) in which you served is helpful, but not essential. It is always helpful to the VA, although painful for you, to cite the name of a buddy killed in your unit or near you. Appendix A of this book gives you links to sites that list the names of those killed in action, both for Vietnam and the Middle East. Included in Appendix C are examples of VA Forms 21-0781 that resulted in compensation benefits being awarded to veterans without combat awards for post-traumatic stress.

You benefit today from a change in VA law in July 2010. From that time, the veteran claiming PTSD is not required to cite a specific incident. The VA realized, after many years, that a veteran should not be penalized for forgetting the date and place of one trauma among many, or have to cite an incident that, for reasons of his own sanity, he put at the back of the closet shelf of his mind. It is sufficient to state where you were, what you were trained to do, your actual work duties, and what happened to make you fear for your life and safety. Classic non-combat situations include mortar and rocket attacks, convoy duties, combat engineer or Seabee situations, military police patrolling, caring for the dead and wounded, and temporary combat duties, such as urban patrols or perimeter security. The legitimate threat of, or the fear of enemy action is deemed a reasonable stressor for claim purposes under the 2010 change in the law. It is wise to state, "I feared for my life every day I was in Iraq" or similar wording.

You may be handed a VA Form 21-0781 to complete yourself, or your vet rep might write it for you and have you sign it. Do not be tempted to write the "great American novel." The VA wants one well-worded paragraph. It is not necessary to fill up both incident spaces on the form. It is not necessary to give the exact date of the incident, if you cannot recall it. Make it read so that any reasonable person would have the same symptoms as you when faced with the same situation you were in.

Claiming Disabilities in Addition to PTSD?

If you are claiming other disabilities in addition to PTSD on the long VA Form 21-526, be sure that these are health issues you know will be listed in your service treatment records. The VA will chase down your health records, but they will not appreciate dealing with claims for health issues that cannot be proven using your treatment records—PTSD and traumatic brain injury (TBI) being the big exceptions to this. PTSD and TBI are typically not diagnosed on active duty. Another set of health issues that will almost never be reflected in military treatment records are those listed by the VA as presumed from exposure to Agent Orange (See Appendix D of this book). Also, the more conditions you claim, the more time the VA will have to spend working on them. Expect the process to take more than a year in such cases. To speed cases of multiple injuries or conditions, submit any copies of your treatment records you may have with the claim. If you do not have your own military treatment records, the VA will locate them in military records. Leave for later the disabilities for which neither you nor your military branch of service has treatment records (again, PTSD, TBI and presumed Agent Orange conditions being the most notable exceptions).

Protect Your Date of Claim with an Informal Claim

A lack of consistency in procedures exists, unfortunately, among vet reps. Some will require a veteran without a combat award to bring in a diagnosis of post-traumatic stress from a VA clinic, Vet Center, or from a private doctor before he/she will write up your claim. If you otherwise like or trust this vet rep, or if that office is convenient to you, have that vet rep write an Informal Claim, or write it yourself. The Informal Claim does not have to be on a particular form. Just write a letter. An Informal Claim states your name, address, phone number, Social Security Number, branch of military service and dates of service. State that you are claiming post-traumatic stress disorder, traumatic brain injury, or any other conditions that show up in your military treatment records. Have your vet rep fax it to your nearest VA Regional Office or mail it yourself. Keep a copy of your letter, or of the fax return message. Your claim will be dated from the date the VA receives your Informal Claim. Prepare your stressor statement while you are waiting to file your formal claim.

The VCAA (Veterans Claims Assistance Act) Letter

At some point in the processing of the claim, when the VA receives all the proper forms, you will receive a VA letter and a stack of still more forms. This letter causes untold confusion among veterans, because it plugs PTSD, TBI and presumed conditions such as Agent Orange disorders into standard form-letter wording asking you to prove that your disability resulted from military service. The circumstances of your service are sufficient to prove that all of these disabilities are from military service. You do not have to prove it, unless the VA has a specific question about your particular service in a war zone or your combat stressor incident. Within that packet is a one-page "VCAA" form with two check blocks. Unless you have further treatment records, or unless the VA asks some specific question of you, check the upper block, "I have sent all I have in support of my claim," sign it, and send it in. Put the rest of the forms into a recycling bin.

At the time of this writing, some regional offices are using a variation of this letter having one check block. The acronym "VCAA" does not appear. This form letter requires that you check the block, acknowledging that you have sent the VA all you want to submit in support of your claim. If you have any other evidence to submit, attach it to this form with a cover letter stating what you are sending.

Who Decides If You Have a Disability?

You will read books and Internet scuttlebutt about the uncaring, cold bureaucrats at the VA. These folks are human civil servants. They're not in it for money; no one gets rich on a federal salary. An adjudicator at your nearest VA Regional Office applies VA law to your specific case. The evidence called for has to be there. He is bound by adjudication and rating manuals, and by current VA policy on specific issues. He has a pile of claims folders on each side of his desk, and he is surrounded by file cabinets with many more folders. He works them one by one. He may or may not be a veteran. An adjudicator I met turned out to be a former combat medic. Only rarely should you need to visit your Regional Office. A visit should only be necessary for an appeal or other hearing. The adjudicator and rating specialists are not allowed contact with individual veterans. This distance keeps the system honest. They can only work with the facts you give them.

Claims do not always go smoothly or as planned. In six years I have had a few claims lost, and I have had the national records repository in St. Louis fail to act on requests for medals and records. Both are inexcusable, but rare. In one case, a claim was sent through a lengthy appeal process because the VA would not acknowledge that the veteran's unit was indeed where he said it was in Vietnam. I was able to prove his case with a Google search of his unit. The VA office tasked with tracking down military unit information had failed to find information that an inexperienced vet rep found quickly. The veteran was made to suffer for that office's lack of diligent effort. Unfortunately, claims adjudication can vary among regional offices and even among individual adjudicators in the same office. As a vet rep, I have had to find additional evidence, letters home, or even statements from those who served in the veteran's unit to reopen denied claims. For this reason, your vet rep will be a very good person to know.

If your Vet Center counselor or VA doctor says you have PTSD, you have it. However, this is not a guarantee of VA compensation. The VA is a bureaucracy, bound by very specific guidelines. Fear of the Russians on maneuvers in Germany, fearing a North Korean attack in 1980 that never occurred, or feeling traumatized by the rigors of military life will probably not get you compensation money. The PTSD diagnosis means you should keep going to your Vet Center or VA Clinic for treatment, whether or not it is followed up by money.

Keep Up Your VA Clinic or Vet Center Treatment

The important reason you are at the Vet Center or VA Clinic is to get help. Vet Centers vary to the extent to which they become involved in the claims process, but they exist to treat PTS. The money you receive from a successful claim is nice, but this place is all about healing. Counselors have proven techniques to lead you to realizing truths that will help you. They don't lecture you or preach to you. Their questioning is meant to lead you to reach certain conclusions. You may be invited to participate in "group." There you will listen to other vets' experiences and share your own. The group facilitator will talk about strategies for dealing with PTS, giving the guys' experiences as situations where these strategies might apply. The Vet Center might offer relaxation techniques, yoga, meditation, tai chi, Anger Management classes, and help for your spouse.

The "C&P" Exam

After pouring your heart out to your Vet Center counselor or doctor, and having filed a claim, you will be asked to go, usually to the nearest VA Medical Center, for an exam by a doctor specializing in PTS. At this point, the medical (or psychological) treatment and the VA claims process come together. Being asked to go to a "C&P" (compensation and pension) exam is an indication that the VA recognizes your combat award, or believes what you told them about the incident(s) that caused your PTSD. The C&P doctor's time with you might seem brief, but they know the right questions to ask. In most cases, you don't have to play-act some "crazy vet" scenario. If you don't normally walk around in a fatigue shirt full of patches, don't do it for this exam. If you don't feel like shaving, then don't. Be who you are. Do not smile at this doctor, and do not be sidetracked into talking about a hobby, your kids or a memorable vacation. After this interview, wait patiently. It may be months before you are finally told in an Award Letter that you are a certain percent disabled and that you will receive a certain amount in a monthly check.

I must be honest with you and inform you that inconsistencies can occur in the VA's C&P exam process. It is important to talk with other vets and find out which doctors are "PTSD friendly." This is just one good reason for not isolating yourself from other veterans. Returning veterans usually fare better on C&P exams than veterans of earlier wars, because your memories are fresh and the doctors tend to be more empathetic toward you.

You May Receive Compensation Money

Do not make financial plans based on compensation money. Most VA Regional Offices are severely understaffed. Your money may be long in coming, over a year in most cases. Do not let anyone tell you the percent, or a money value your claim will be worth. Every claim is different.

Is money a cure for PTSD? Actually, no amount of money can properly compensate you for what you have suffered, for what you have lost, or for the years your country has neglected to make treatment and benefit information available to you. The legal remedy is called "to make the plaintiff whole." No amount of money can do that. It may, however, supplement your income to make up for the work you cannot do, or have not been able to do.

Once you are 70% disabled (40% of which must be from a single disability, PTSD being one), you will be invited to apply for the 100% compensation rate based on individual unemployability (I/U). This means that you are declaring yourself to be unable to obtain and hold gainful employment. One Vet Center I know of urges most of its clients to file for I/U. The pitfall here is that the veteran may be, in order to get nearly $3,000 tax-free per month, imposing an idleness onto himself that turns out not to be good for him. Should a cabinet-maker stop making drawers with perfect dovetail joints, if that is what he does well? Should a teacher stop teaching, if she could do the same work part-time to lessen the load? These are questions you should ask yourself before settling on being termed "unemployable." Might it not be better to settle for half the compensation money in exchange for continuing to feel—and to be—productive?

Once you have been rated, and assigned a percentage of disability, you will begin receiving monthly checks. This amount is US income tax free. At this time, you should call your local VA toll-free number and request letters granting you 10-point veterans' preference for civil service employment, and letters you can use for free or reduced-fee state and national park visits, hunting and fishing licenses, and tax reductions and other benefits your state may or may not offer. If you have never checked in at a VA hospital or clinic, take your award letter to the eligibility desk. You will be enrolled in the VA Health Care System, even if you have never before used VA Health Care.

If You Disagree With the Outcome of Your Claim

Occasionally, vets will receive a 0% rating. This is NOT a denial of your claim. It is saying that the VA does not deem the problem to be significant enough to pay you money, but it acknowledges that the issue is service connected. The classic example is an appendectomy scar. It does not in any way diminish your ability to earn a living, unless, perhaps, you are contemplating a career modeling swimwear. A 0% is, in some cases, a "foot in the door." Another classic example is hearing loss. Though initially rated 0%, this may get worse with age. If you think this is happening to you, get a current audiology test and bring it to your vet rep.

Any VA compensation claim can be reopened if the symptoms are significantly worse, or if conditions based on employability or health needs change. The form for this is the one-page VA Form 21-526B. But be sure that your claimed conditions are, in fact, worse. Gather your treatment records to present to the VA, or inform the VA about what VA facility is treating you. You can also reopen a claim that has been denied if you can offer evidence the VA has not yet seen. New and material evidence is always the best way to handle a denial.

Claims can be denied on points of law. All types of cancer are not recognized as Agent Orange related. Sleep apnea is not automatically considered as secondary to PTSD, unless your doctor makes that connection. If you claim a disability that has a poor chance of a successful claim, do not use that denial as a springboard for righteous anger. If you struggle with PTS, you have enough anger to deal with.

Multiple conditions claimed result in multiple disability rating percentages. For example, 50% for PTSD, 20% for diabetes, 10% for tinnitus, and 10% for diabetic neuropathy in each foot totals 70%. The percentages do not add up arithmetically. The VA figures your total percentage using its combining rating scheme. They are not cheating you.

You have the right to appeal any VA decision. Consider the appeal process only as a last resort. Always enlist the services of an experienced vet rep if you decide to appeal your case. The appeal process is lengthy.

Non Service-Connected Disability and Death Pensions

Do not confuse VA Compensation with VA Pension. The disability pension is for wartime veterans the VA deems to be permanently and totally disabled, because of health issues or being 65 or older. The veteran must have very low income, or such severe medical care expenses as to significantly or totally offset his or her income. A widow who has lost the protection and companionship of her veteran husband may file for death pension. Like the veteran, her income must be very low, and/or her health care costs must be very high. Your father or mother may be eligible for this benefit, whether as a veteran or as a surviving spouse. Ask your vet rep.

Room for Improvement

I am advising you to "make peace with the VA," but I struggle with several issues that I myself have trouble making peace with. First, the agency is badly understaffed, not the fault of the VA. What was our country thinking to embark on two simultaneous wars and then not plan for veterans coming home from those wars needing help? State and local veterans services agencies are chronically understaffed as well. Adding health conditions related to Agent Orange exposure in Viet Nam and making the burden of proof for PTSD easier to bear has resulted in many more claims. These changes were just, correct and long overdue. Allowances should have been made for processing such claims.

Secondly, inconsistencies in claims adjudication, ratings and in C&P exam evaluations are causing confusion among veterans, and in some cases causing real damage. Additionally, veterans are treated inconsistently at Vet Centers and Clinics. A Marine combat veteran was told at a Vet Center in Florida that he was a loser who had ruined his life and was trying to extort money from the VA. When he came to my office with a 10% compensation rating for anxiety, I welcomed him home, to California where he was born, and where his claim for PTSD would receive fair treatment. A competent vet rep, the San Jose Vet Center, the Oakland Regional Office, and a sympathetic C&P exam doctor cooperated to correct his VA compensation problem. Within the same urban California VA system, one doctor is generous with the numerical scoring he gives of PTSD symptoms, and another doctor on the same staff has told at least one combat veteran he does not have PTSD. A Huey pilot who landed troops in a mined landing zone and had to Medevac them out in a shredded helicopter was told that, since he had been married 40 years to the same woman, went to church, and had hobbies, he did not have PTSD. His case is under appeal.

Veterans consider VA claims, especially for PTSD, TBI, Agent Orange diseases and Gulf War Syndrome, to be validation that they went to war, suffered for their service, and that they are, in fact, home. To deny or to low-ball a legitimate claim is to deny the veteran the validation he seeks. A denial might, additionally, deprive a veteran of VA health care. A low-ball rating might deprive him/her of a higher level of VA care.

Hearing loss and tinnitus are issues dealt with capriciously by the VA. A WWII Army Air Forces pilot was, quite rightly, granted service connection for his hearing loss and tinnitus, although he never went on sick call for it. Claims from an artillery veteran, a mortar crewman and an aircraft carrier flight-deck technician were denied. Most of us do not report hearing loss and tinnitus in service. I would have been laughed out of the aid station had I reported my ears ringing after the rocket attack that nearly hit me. At the very least, hearing loss and tinnitus should be conceded for any combat veteran. We do not wear hearing protection when we have to be alert and hear orders clearly.

Finally, in this age of computerization of eligibility data and medical treatment records, we should be able to expect the VA to treat us without question when we appear at a distant clinic or hospital when visiting family or on vacation. Yet, I have heard of veterans being denied treatment outside of their home state, even when handing over their VA medical system card. I would expect this situation to be corrected.

No other country in history has taken better care of veterans than our own. Lapses and inconsistencies have existed. When these are called to the attention of our elected representatives, they can be addressed, although change is often slow in coming. The VA's facilities, its budget and its staffing deserve to be protected and preserved, regardless of politics. VA care and monetary benefits do not deserve to be called an "entitlement program." As imperfect as the agency can be, it is the only VA we have.

CHAPTER 9

When We Don't Treat Each Other As Brothers and Sisters

My friend had been in Marine Corps basic training only a few days, in 1966. A drill sergeant beat a trainee senseless in a stairwell in front of other Marine recruits. This made no sense, in a group of boys who were intimidated anyway, and who were only trying to do what was expected of them.

A sailor was forced to a remote part of his ship, anally assaulted with a foreign object, and was told he would be thrown off the ship if he reported it, and that his parents would be told he was lost at sea.

A female colleague of mine was sexually harassed, both verbally and physically, by a supervisor in the Coast Guard. She adapted a defensive tactic used by prison inmates, of immediate, forceful retaliation, hitting the NCO full in the face with her hand. She was disciplined for it, but earned the guy's respect. She should not have had to do this to co-exist peacefully with her male supervisor.

A victim of a gang rape incident in an Air Force barracks was counseled to keep quiet about it. Decades passed before she sought VA treatment of PTS.

In all of the cases cited above, the VA awarded or is likely to award compensation, although, in the male-on-male situation, the victim's symptoms are being called "depression and anxiety."

Both men and women can be raped in military service. If I can summarize some things common to the incidents I know about, it's that the person to whom this happens is threatened with force or death if he/she reports it. Also, people in "helper" positions, such as medical people or even chaplains, advise silence, to "make it easier on yourself."

The military is only a reflection of the rest of American society. Since sexual harassment happens in the business, academic, and bureaucratic worlds, we can expect it to occur in the military.

A salient feature, however, of the military that makes this so troubling is the authority structure. Other people have absolute power of life and death over a service member. An army military police supervisor, in bending a female subordinate to his will, told her she could be put on street patrol in Baghdad, instead of continuing in the office job for which she was trained.

The other troubling aspect of this behavior is the way the military tries to portray itself as more disciplined, more moral, or more righteous than the society at large. Total submission and obedience are seen as the highest virtues, part of the discipline that should be imposed on the restless, misbehaved youth in our society. The problem with this is that it is a ready-made opportunity for people with predatory intentions. Rape and other forms of abuse are not so much about sexual gratification as about power over other people. These predatory people are no better than the clergy, teachers, coaches, and doctors who make the headlines with abuse of the trust we place in them.

In spite of the lip service to "values" in the past decades, this still goes on in the military. Perpetrators go unpunished, and victims go unheard and uncompensated. Those in positions of leadership who allow and condone this are no better than their civilian counterparts. If you are going to claim to be better, you have to BE better. A young person enlists in the US military expecting to do meaningful and important work with professionals. We hope to take our place among them, by earning their respect and trust. We are blindsided when these professionals turn out to be thugs. The outrage develops into PTS, or worse, PTSD.

Once out of the military, a veteran may file a claim for the effects of brutal behavior, or of sexual harassment. The Department of Veterans Affairs even has a special PTS stressor incident reporting form (VA Form 21-0781a) on which to document the incident.

Include this form with your VA Form 21-526, claiming post-traumatic stress disorder.

Listening to a young woman talk about a rape incident recently, I was too angry to do my midday gym routine, because I was afraid of hitting the weights too hard and hurting myself. This girl, the age of my daughter, was not treated as a sister, but as a piece of meat, for someone's entertainment. A man or woman does not have to have PTS to be outraged by hearing of such treatment. A person who has PTS is doubly triggered. I am seeing, in front of me a son or daughter, and a veteran. I remember that I was just the kind of trusting kid this might have happened to. I see the hurt in their eyes. My PTS is triggered and I am angry.

Such cases are one of the nightmares of veterans' advocacy. No person who has come to me with reports like this is lying. Unless the incident was reported to those in authority and the report was documented, the claim may be a difficult one to prove. The veteran then must resort to medical treatment records, statements from someone who knew you and in whom you confided, and documented records of a profound change in behavior, demeanor or job performance after the incident.

Neither combat nor PTS is an excuse for abuse. A man, especially a leader, who looks at a female serving with him and, instead of offering her safety and protection, sees her only as a potential object of gratification, does not deserve to be in our presence.

A leader who ignores the problem, placing his career ahead of the welfare of his subordinate, does not deserve a leadership position because he has shown he cannot handle leadership responsibility. If he is powerless to prevent the abuse, he can at least see that justice is done.

At the time of this writing, our Congress is wrestling with questions of legal jurisdiction in sexual assault cases, because the military's Uniform Code of Military Justice seems to be too often ignored or circumvented. A VA doctor recently told me he is deeply disturbed by the reports of sexual assault told to him by his patients. Women who have served in Iraq told me that they went to the latrine or to the shower in groups, because alone they were subjected to attack. They risked health problems from holding bodily waste until they could go to the bathroom safely. A respected activist in the veterans' peace movement, former Army Colonel Ann Wright, said recently that the number of women raped in military service during the OIF/OEF (Operation Iraqi Freedom/Operation Enduring Freedom) years may be as high as one in three. As a vet rep, I cannot confirm or refute this figure, but I can tell you that I dealt with far too many of these cases. If this estimate is even close, I must recommend, as a former soldier and as a veterans advocate, that women not enlist until the military commits itself to protect women and to see that justice is done when they are not protected.

The VA provides female victims with therapy, individually and as part of a support group. As of this writing, such groups for men, although promised, have never materialized. The VA Palo Alto Health Care System, a leader in high-quality VA care, somehow cannot find the money and people to care for these decent, trusting men.

As men, we must take no comfort in any notion that the atrocities of the militaries of other countries seem worse than our own. In Vietnam, we tolerated violence against Vietnamese women, and we willingly participated in shameful human trafficking operations. These young women with whom we consorted in bars and on our "R and R" (rest-and-relaxation) trips were forced into prostitution by poverty. These girls appeared to be consenting adults, but, in truth, there are no happy hookers. To the extent to which we men consider ourselves to be entitled to the sexual services of women, we are treating them shamefully. We felt entitled to these young women's services because we had paid for them. Like warriors from other times and other places, all of us probably had some notion of entitlement to the women in this country where we did not want to be. We saw them as being of the "enemy", or as vanquished, helpless people. We treated them in ways we would not have treated a college classmate. We did what we did because we could, and because everyone else was doing it. Paying these women for their services and treating them with reasonable kindness does not absolve us of the shame of participating in human trafficking. Smitty, a guy in my unit, got it right. He put the girl he had hired onto a train and marched her back to her village and family. We teased him when he told us about his R and R experience, but we all knew he was right.

War brings out the worst in all of us. However, war and military service are not to blame for the assaults on women that are all too prevalent in our society. We men need to examine this deep-rooted notion of entitlement to sexual access to women. We need to deal with it on a personal level, as fathers, bothers and as friends.

CHAPTER 10

Bad Discharge

A less-than-honorable discharge from military service will cause a veteran difficulty obtaining VA services and VA education benefits. Additionally, since employers often want to see your military discharge, an other-than-honorable discharge might prevent you from getting a job. At the time of this writing, the least punitive discharge, the General Under Honorable Conditions, will keep the veteran from using his GI Bill benefit, the post 9-11 GI Bill, or the Montgomery GI Bill into which the veteran made contributions.

For active-duty people, the obvious advice is not to get a bad discharge. You know what your military branch expects, and you know what the penalties are likely to be for breaking the rules. The military must impose penalties for such offenses as desertion, dereliction of duty, or rendering oneself incapable of doing one's military job because of alcohol or drug use. The military cannot tolerate people failing to show up for work or being too stoned to work.

That said, all branches of the military have been too eager to slap a service member with a punitive discharge without regard for his or her mental or emotional problems, family issues, and, worst of all, acting out or misbehavior with post-traumatic stress disorder or traumatic brain injury, often after combat or after multiple combat assignments.

For the veteran's services representative, the most difficult discharges to contest are those resulting from offenses such as mistreatment of or assaults on fellow service members, extended periods of absence without leave, and patterned, persistent misbehavior. Many government entities offering veterans' services do not assist with discharge upgrades. My own county ordered me not to attempt them, even after I successfully got a discharge upgraded to Honorable through the California Army National Guard by submitting a prior Honorable Discharge and two diagnoses of PTSD. My supervisor made it clear I would be doing such upgrade work from my garage if he caught me attempting another upgrade from my office. My county, however, was right in one respect; discharge upgrades often require legal expertise that we vet reps are unlikely to have.

You should definitely attempt to upgrade a less-than-honorable discharge. You should get help for this. Your state or county veterans services rep, a veterans services organization (usually co-located with your VA Regional Office), some chapters of the American Red

Cross, peace or civil rights groups, local legal aid and private attorneys are possible sources of help.

First, get a copy of your service personnel records. You and your representative must have the proceedings by which you were given this kind of discharge.

If less than fifteen years have elapsed since your discharge, file DD Form 293 and all pertinent documents, with your own statement of your argument, to the address given on the form for your service. Your service's Discharge Review Board (DRB) consists of five military officers, probably Lt. Colonels or Colonels. You normally will appear in person, with your representative. Traveling boards will come to your area, but you may travel to Washington, D.C. for your hearing.

If your discharge is older than fifteen years, file DD Form 149 with the Board for the Correction of Military Records (BCMR). The BCMR consists of three to five high-ranking civilian employees of your branch of service. If the discharge is a Bad Conduct Discharge or a Dishonorable Discharge, you would file DD Form 149 with the BCMR regardless of elapsed time.

Concurrently with any attempt to upgrade your discharge, apply with the VA for the benefit you want, whether it is health care, education, or consideration of a disability claim. A veteran with post–traumatic stress disorder would ask the VA Health Care System for treatment for that problem. Along with your application for health benefits on VA Form 10-10EZ, attach a copy of your discharge, any previous Honorable Discharge, your personnel records, and, especially, any mental health clinic or VA Vet Center records showing a diagnosis of PTSD.

For VA education benefits, apply on VA Form 22-1990. Attach the same records as with the one for health benefits. Write a statement that you are in need of education as part of your healing process.

Apply for disability compensation on VA Form 21-526. If you are claiming PTSD, or TBI, by all means attach any diagnosis you may have received, from the military, from the VA, or from private treatment.

In all cases, the VA will notify you that they are making an eligibility determination, based on the character of your discharge. Submit any statement of your own and any evidence you think might help your case. A statement from your treatment professional might carry a bit of weight. The VA might grant the benefit you seek. However, the VA cannot upgrade your discharge.

In the light of recent publicity about the incidence of PTSD among combat veterans, we stand a chance of favorable outcomes of discharge upgrades with the main extenuating circumstance being PTSD and prolonged or multiple combat tours. Traumatic brain injury (TBI) might be still another extenuating circumstance.

A strategy favored by many veterans' advocates is the model citizen defense. You are working on your education, with or without the benefit of the GI Bill. You are working to support yourself and your wife and child(ren), you are a volunteer on civic or veterans projects, or you submit statements from people who attest to your good character.

Still another punitive action occurs with service members who have been treated for mental disorders. Their discharge, although Honorable in character, will have an entry at the bottom of the DD214 of "Personality Disorder." Use the model citizen defense, a personal statement, character references, firm diagnoses of any mental disorder you might have, and any pressing circumstances in which such an entry on your DD214 might be seen as a stigma. For example, one veteran with a sensitive US Civil Service job requiring a security clearance appealed to the BCMR and asked successfully that the "Personality Disorder" entry be removed from his record, citing the position he already held and the need for a security clearance.

Much of this anguish could be avoided if the military would resolve to treat combat veterans with fairness and compassion. As a citizen and a veteran, am I asking too much to expect that consideration and compassion be extended to veterans of combat, people who have suffered abuse, and people who have sought care for mental illness? Must the mental anguish resulting in having seen the innocent die in hideous ways, or from praying over the shattered body of a fallen brother be met with punitive action? What kind of twisted values favors punishment over treatment, judgment over compassion and punitive discharges in exchange for faithful combat service? What kind of military do we have? More disturbingly, to what extent are these injustices a reflection of the rest of our country?

CHAPTER 11

Citizen Soldier

You have been to war, and have been touched by its effects on you. How much of your energies will be spent in the coming of years dealing with the war depends, I think, on the intensity of your combat experience. You will deal with PTS on some level. At the very least, the experience of going to war will always be part of who you are.

At almost any gathering of veterans, you will see people who seem to be defining themselves in terms of having been to war. They wear hats or bits of uniform with unit affiliations, flags, or political opinions on them. You will see this in the grocery store checkout line and at the hardware store, as well as at events for veterans.

You can choose to wear your service on your sleeve or tuck it away, fitting it in with all the other roles we take on in life, as a spouse, a parent, a tradesperson or a professional. Your service has a place in your life. It will fit somewhere. You have control over the importance you attach to it, how it fits in who you are, and the face you present to other people in your life. Place it in its proper perspective, so that it receives just the right amount of weight, and it will be part of the best you have to give.

In my work with veterans, I find that many of you underestimate the value of your service on your resumes. Even as an E4, you had some responsibility in your own job, and also for the work, welfare and safety of others around you. You successfully completed training for a complex, important job. As an NCO, you had to do counseling to help fellow soldiers deal with problems on the job and perhaps in their lives. You dealt with complex problem-solving, and in some cases you made decisions in life-and-death situations. If you were recognized by the military for your job performance, such as your service's Commendation or Achievement Medal, or received a combat award, it should show up on your resume. Your pride in having completed a period of military service should show. Our country's overall attitude toward military service is much improved over what it was in 1973. Employers are interested in what you did and how well you did it.

You have a GI Bill benefit that is unparalleled in our country's history. Mine in 1971-1978 saw me though a Master's degree. Yours can take you there and more, but with a far more generous stipend that includes living expenses, tuition and books. This chance at an education is the best thing that can happen to you, just as it was for my father's generation and for my own. Many of you enlisted because of these education benefits. You put life, limb and sanity on the line to earn this opportunity.

Give some thought to the locality in which you want to study and its attitude toward education. Look at your state's funding for higher education. Can people of student age get into the classes they need to graduate? Do not expect any college to give you favorable treatment over other students. Check out the cost of college and the availability of classes in any other state in which you might consider living.

If you have little idea of what you want to study, you are right in there with most of your buddies, and with me in 1971. If you have no previous college experience, consider taking an Associate's Degree program, or a couple of courses at a time at the community college level. This will prove to you that you can do college work.

Don't expect it to be easy. These courses may expose weaknesses in your writing or math skills. Get help. I had academic problems. I found college instructors and professors to be interested and helpful. Their red marks on your papers, quizzes, and exams are a wake-up call. These people will make you a better writer or make you competent in math, if you let them. Don't be surprised if your professor is a Vietnam or Gulf War vet.

You will find the interest in life that "blows your hair back"—that, when you find it, you realize that it is what you really want to do. Keep an open mind, because you never know what it will be. I know a female Iraq vet who has trained to be an electrician. There is no reason men cannot be competent, compassionate nurses and therapists of all kinds. Give a career in education some thought. You might make a difference in young people's lives.

At the time of this writing, the US Department of Veterans Affairs is looking for OIF/OEF (Operation Iraqi Freedom/Operation Enduring Freedom) veterans as counselors in the treatment of post-traumatic stress at VA Vet Centers. What your degree is in matters less for this than experience in counseling, especially counseling in the military. Counselors typically have a Masters in Social Work or Psychology, or even a Ph.D. But if your degree is on the Bachelors level, apply anyway if you have the experience.

Consider learning a trade. I know auto mechanics, plumbers, roofers, drywall installers, photographers, dental lab techs and others who run honest, competent businesses. When I asked a local plumber the reasons for his obvious success (new home, nice car, etc.), he said, "It's not rocket science, Doug. I come when I say I'm going to come, and do what I say I am going to do. If I make a mistake, I own up to it and come back and make it right. Word gets around. And I charge what everyone else charges."

Take some business administration and accounting courses, because as a tradesman you are running a business.

You may be like me and not find a specific career goal until later in life. But any degree in any major tells a prospective employer that this energetic young person can finish what he/she starts, can handle scheduling and prioritizing, can communicate well in written and spoken English, and perhaps in another language, too.

Be flexible within your career goal. I majored in Anthropology for my B.A., but soon realized that I was not going to be a professor of anthropology. The cluttered office and the tweed jacket were not to be. Yet, not a day goes by that I don't use what I learned in those classes about human behavior and thinking—both to relate to veterans of various ethnic, educational and economic backgrounds and to relate to family, friends and associates. My M.A. is in Education, and I find myself doing adult education.

A liberal arts education, and even the "distribution courses" required early in college, let you see into the many windows in the academic disciplines. Choose to work in one, or take what you want from several or all of them. Meet your foreign language study requirement eagerly, as you will have an inside track when travelling to the country where that language is spoken.

Many of you, especially in the Guard and Reserve, already have your degree. Great career changes are possible for you, too. Take the Law School Aptitude Test (LSAT). Don't, as I did, get stuck with a TV drama view of law practice. If you are good with the language, aren't intimidated by tough academic work, and have a love of justice, law might be just what you've been looking for. If you cannot imagine yourself arguing a case in a courtroom, there are many corporations, government agencies and non-profits that have legal staffs. A law degree is nearly essential for public office. You must be able to deal with issues of considerable complexity, and read and comprehend an incredible amount of material.

Other advanced degrees in any number of psychology, counseling, health administration, and ministerial fields can prepare you for the helping professions.

Your local (city or county), state, and US federal Civil Service are open to you as a veteran. In the federal system, you get 5 points of preference simply as a veteran, and 10 points as a disabled veteran. Go to www.usajobs.gov and apply for any federal job for which you believe yourself qualified and for which you would relocate. State and local governments all have human resources websites easily accessible by using a search engine.

Apply again and again, because it is highly unlikely you will succeed the first time. Accept a job that requires less preparation than you have. When I worked as a VA benefits counselor at a VA Hospital in Virginia, I got into a conversation with a guy sweeping the hall floor whom I had never seen before. He said,"Yeah, this is a GS-2 job, very low pay grade, very little responsibility. I have a degree. Watch me."

Some months later, I met him coming down the same hallway in a three-piece suit, carrying a briefcase. He got his "foot in the door," did his job well, and applied from within the system for other jobs for which his degree qualified him.

Federal civil service jobs include many within the US military system of schools, and many administrative jobs, also. The civil service in general welcomes veterans, and the military system of civilian workers is particularly open to them. Your job experience in the military may make you eminently qualified for some jobs. My son served seven years as a supply sergeant, came out with a disability, and has served in the US Civil Service as a ROTC unit supply specialist, an ammunition specialist and as an overseer of contractors on a major military base.

In some cases, your experience will speak louder than your college degrees. You must, however, reconcile any lingering personal ambivalence about military solutions to political problems before you commit yourself to the military as your civilian job. If they give you a job, you owe them the most conscientious service you are able to give, no less, regardless of your political views.

Certain political factions in our country question the need for government regulation and oversight, and so question the expense of staffing a civil service. But I think that the people of San Bruno, California would have liked someone to inspect the gas pipeline there before it exploded in September 2010, destroying homes and killing several people. I would think the people who work in coal mines or who send husbands and sons down into the earth to work in them would rather someone monitor methane levels than not. Competent oversight of Gulf oil drilling might have prevented the oil spill tragedy. In each case, private industry failed to regulate itself.

All this said, don't expect any civil service system—federal, state, or local—to be the exclusive domain of veterans. Civil service on all levels welcomes women and minority groups it believes are disadvantaged in some way. Look at this as an opportunity to get to know these other workers, and to learn from them. One of my co-workers in local civil service is not a veteran, but a young woman, college educated, of Mexican descent. She is an excellent veterans' service representative, because she has heart. She cares about the people she serves.

Finally, as a career, consider becoming a vet rep. The VA still has contact representatives, also, but that function has largely been turned over to the states and counties. In California, you go to a county vet rep to file a claim. Check your state and county job listings. Also, look at private veterans' organizations (the American Legion, Veterans of Foreign Wars, Amvets, Military Order of the Purple Heart, Paralyzed Veterans of America, Blinded Veterans of America) for vet rep jobs. You will generally need a college education, or at least a solid history of being able to deal with a complex body of law, since you will be interpreting these laws to people of all educational and cultural backgrounds.

Any of these organizations would jump at an educated Iraq or Afghanistan vet who can relate to buddies on a personal level. You do their claims paperwork, and point them in the right direction for help from other agencies. These jobs can pay fairly well, and they pay even better when you become a veterans services officer, in charge of other vet reps. Be ready to prove combat for the veterans who experienced life-threatening situations but who do not have combat awards. Be willing to do the necessary computer searches for unit histories for vets who cannot do it themselves.

Be thick-skinned when necessary, because you will not make everyone happy. This may not be the ideal job for someone who has PTS. You may be affected by the experiences of other veterans. If I had known my own PTS would be heightened by working with veterans who struggle with PTS, I would still have chosen to be a vet rep. I have found I have to be careful, however, to take care of myself, intellectually, emotionally and physically, in all the ways outlined in this book.

In the light of our country's, and the world's, economic crisis we should all try to manage our family's micro-economy. I mention this because I have seen the effects of uncontrolled spending, and also of the easy credit borrowing that makes this possible. Credit card companies are owned by banks. We can too easily find ourselves lining the pockets of the very banks and financial speculators who have looted our country's economy. We too easily become slaves to consumer debt, to the point of jeopardizing our very homes and our children's education.

For all of us, the questions, "Do we really need to buy this?" and "Is this necessary?" are a constant struggle. Consider freeing yourself of this burden by buying just what you need and no more and by limiting credit card debt to emergencies.

As a veteran, you have put yourselves in harm's way, sacrificed time away from your family, and perhaps have suffered wounds to body and spirit. No one has more of a right to speak up, on any issue, not just those involving going to war. You have gone to places, met people and seen and done things your fellow citizens cannot imagine. They need to hear your point of view.

I can promise you that your views on your war, my war, or war in general will differ from those of some of your fellow veterans. Given our mutual respect for such military concepts as chain of command and civility, we will agree to disagree on some issues and to argue respectfully. We are all the sum total of our experience and memories. Your point of view is as valid as mine. If it were up to me, none of you would have invaded or occupied Afghanistan or Iraq. It was not up to me. I respect the fact that you considered the reasons our leaders gave you for going to war to be worth your life.

In our country's political history, we have never agreed to be ruled by monarchs or political entities that have absolute power. Our political history consists of working out our differences, sometimes painfully, about what part and level of our government holds what power.

We fought a bitter civil war, in which my great-great grandfather was killed, and from which my great grandfather came back shattered. Neither of these poor dirt farmers had anything to gain from the institution of slavery. I do not think the issue was slavery so much as it was the prospect of a strong federal government making economic decisions weighing heavily on agricultural states.

As a nation, we have still not resolved these basic questions. Is it the responsibility of our federal government to provide health care to the poor and unemployed, albeit at considerable cost to those of us who can afford to pay for our own? Is it the responsibility of the federal government to regulate banking and other commerce to protect us from usurious interest rates, and risky investment? Do corporations hold such power over our lives that the government must take on the task of regulating their behavior? Is technology so powerful that it cannot be left to market forces? Are pesticides, for example, so potentially lethal that government oversight must proscribe their application?

How valid is our long-held view that we Americans practice "democracy," and that we are "bringing democracy" to other countries when we embark on military adventures? The influence of Big Money over important financial and policy issues has led to a disastrous lack of oversight over banking and speculation. The result has been the loss of jobs and the crash of the world's economy. Reasonable regulation of business that would have contributed to the public safety and welfare has been pre-empted by lobbyists' influences over our lawmakers. Are we claiming to be the champions of a democracy we do not in fact practice ourselves?

As a democracy we tolerate extremist thought, expression, and behavior. We do not practice censorship. We welcome freedom of expression. When as much as possible is out in the open, then we can choose for ourselves where our beliefs fall. For this reason, I do not fear the Internet. The younger generation is savvy enough to recognize extremist nonsense. If anything, the Internet is another means of expression. Blogging is still another way to get our legitimate concerns out for others to read. Governments that fear open expression have some control agenda running in the background.

Join your fellow citizens in wrestling with these issues. Too few of us Vietnam veterans actively participated in government, and in civil discourse. Too few of us went to law school. Do your part in making our democracy work.

We have probably all had supervisors or commanders we did not like. In the military, however, we respect the office that that person holds. When we disagree, we do it respectfully, and accept the outcome. As citizens, our elected representatives and President deserve the same respect we showed our military leaders when we were in the service. Shouting down a speaker who has the floor, or carrying lethal firepower to a political rally is embarrassing—and dangerous—to all of us.

Extremism is over the top when it declares that those who disagree with the points of view expressed deserve to be killed, meet with corporal punishment or otherwise be silenced. The 1950's McCarthy era was a time when influential people among our elected representatives decided that people holding certain beliefs were a "threat" to our country's welfare and morals. Punitive actions were taken against their livelihoods and the offices they held.

Extremism is perceived as "over the top" when it is far out of line with the common beliefs of those hearing or reading it. During my active duty in Japan, a base commander decreed that bathtub appliqués in the shape of flowers on the private cars of military personnel were "subversive" and would not be tolerated. Even the military police would not enforce his absurd edict.

Never should we allow the military we served and love to be used in the support of extremism. In the 1970's, while our country was enjoying "flower power" and a resurgence of creativity on all fronts, I was distressed and embarrassed when asked by Japanese college students if the Kent State massacre of students by the Ohio Army National Guard was how my country's democracy dealt with dissent. During the peace demonstrations of the Bush Administration, a HMMWV-mounted ultra-sound "crowd control" weapon was paraded about, manned by army personnel. I saw this as a veiled threat, as something that might be used against peace demonstrations during the current wars. During the years of dictatorship in Argentina, that country's navy held dissidents without trial and executed them. Mostly young people, they were drugged and thrown out of helicopters into the ocean with weights tied to them. On certain days of the month, you can see their mothers marching silently in the main plaza in Buenos Aires. Most recently, the government of Syria has unleashed military technology and firepower on its civilian population.

As citizens we will be called upon to wrestle with the issue of the conduct of war being removed from public knowledge, scrutiny and oversight. It will be all too easy to sit back and allow, as we have already, abduction, torture, secret prisons, government monitoring of our communications and the erosion of our civil liberties. We will be expected to let "the dark side" do its own thing, out of sight and, therefore, not our problem. To the extent to which we still are a democratic republic, military or government action taken in our name is our problem. We have not hesitated to hold the citizens of other countries accountable for the actions of their governments.

The framers of our Constitution were emphatic that the powers of government, including the military, not be turned against our own people. We all took an oath to "support and defend the Constitution against all enemies foreign and domestic." At no time have I been debriefed and told this oath no longer applies. Read, listen and stay informed. Speak when necessary, but don't remain silent.

As citizens, I think we are called upon to wrestle with other constitutional issues. Perhaps because of greater availability of information, we are being blind-sided with issues that we never expected to affect us.

I served with gay soldiers and airmen. Not one of them ever failed to do his best on the job. They lived in our housing complex; we worked with them and partied with them. It is time to welcome them into the military side of our society. Their personal behavior is none of my business. I am confident that the younger generation of Americans will work to see that homophobia joins racism and sexism as features of our society we would like to see gone.

Are you a member of one of several veterans' service organizations? Are you considering working with one of them in a volunteer capacity to help to take care of fellow vets? After telling us after Vietnam that they didn't want us because we didn't win our war, the American Legion and the VFW now want Vietnam vets as members. This would be a good time for veterans of all wars to hold these organizations to their promises to serve and to "leave no veteran behind." These organizations have the facilities and the membership halls to hold "open house" events to inform veterans of such issues as Agent Orange-related disabilities and post-traumatic stress treatment and claims. As members of these organizations, are we willing to walk point for the soldier or marine who walked point for us? Are we willing to take care of the veteran who maintained the aircraft that gave us fire support, or who cooked our meals? Are we willing to hold veterans' organizations to walking the walk, as well as talking the talk?

Regardless of our own similarities or differences, I would like for us to agree on one issue, that of sending yet another generation to war.

It is time to demand honesty from those in our government who would send our sons and daughters to war but not send their own. The old slogans don't work anymore. "Freedom Isn't Free" and this notion that we are fighting for our own or for anyone else's freedom need never again serve as a reason for going to war. Are we ready to read, analyze and consider when we vote, to understand all the issues? Are we willing to ask the right painful questions before we commit young men and women to war? Is this war an absolute last resort? Have all other options been exhausted? Is this war in the true defense of our nation? Is it necessary? Have the reasons for the war been honestly and clearly laid before the American people?

Have we honored the unspoken trust between a soldier and his countrymen—that we will look out for them, care for them, and honor their service? Have we regarded them as our own sons and daughters—not as other people's kids, but as our own? Are they precious young people, each life full of potential, or are they just "troops"?

Are we willing to honor the dead by taking care of the living? Are we willing to spare NO expense in the medical, mental and spiritual care of those who were their buddies in combat? Or are we intent on dismantling the health and benefit system that has served veterans for decades, sneering at the facilities and at the dedicated people who work in them as an "entitlement program"?

As veterans, more is being asked of us. We have been somewhere and have done something. We have seen humankind at its worst. Will we participate in what remains of our democracy, or will we just watch TV? Will we put the education we earned to constructive use, or use PTSD as an excuse to do nothing for the rest of our lives? Are we ready to start defining ourselves as men (and women) in a different way than as warriors? Are we making the effort to love our spouses and to raise our children in loving homes? As veterans who understand the effects of war, are we willing to exercise the most extreme discretion before placing the burden of war and of combat on our children, and our children's generation?

If taking care of those returning from our nation's wars is too expensive, if we cannot hire enough Vet Center counselors and mental health professionals to assist those struggling with PTS, and if we will not hire the claims workers needed to process disability claims, then I can only suggest that we can no longer afford to send our young people to war.

If you can, provide for your children's education so that they do not have to roll the dice of military service and put life, limb, and sanity on the line to earn a college education. If those who clamor for the next war do not send their own children, it is a sure sign that they are pushing the responsibility for waging war onto your children. Keep yours at home.

As Americans, we have much more in common than being veterans. We can sequester ourselves within our society, associating only with other veterans with whom we feel most comfortable, or we can freely associate and learn from others whose experience is different. Instead of defining ourselves as veterans, might we not see ourselves mainly as fathers, mothers, sons, daughters, adult partners, brothers, sisters and friends? The feelings we veterans have for each other should continue, and we must continue to seek justice for fellow veterans in the VA health care and claims arenas. But we are more than veterans, more than people who struggle with post-traumatic stress. We are Americans, taking our place and playing our part in an ever-shrinking economic and political world.

CHAPTER 12

Conclusion

If you have been to war, you may have the symptoms of post-traumatic stress described in Chapter 3. You are not alone, and you are certainly not crazy. Although these symptoms may have had a different name over the years, every soldier who has been in combat, or who has dealt with the aftermath of combat, has experienced the same feelings and emotions as we. If you are a war veteran and you do not have these symptoms, count yourself among the most fortunate. Be vigilant, however, for events that might trigger a flashback, especially as we get older and no longer have full-time jobs to occupy our time and thoughts.

Unlike most nations, ours has a cabinet-level department having responsibility for the diagnosis, treatment and care of those of us who have experienced injury or illness, including post-traumatic stress in military service. That department, the VA, demands specific procedures for obtaining your health care and your disability compensation benefits. I have organized and explained these procedures so that you can navigate the VA system.

You will meet counselors and doctors whose job it is to help you with your symptoms of post-traumatic stress. Show up for appointments, be on time, and engage them in conversation about your concerns. Be willing to explore treatment options your Vet Center or VA Mental Health Clinic offers. Such practices as yoga, tai chi or transcendental meditation have known therapeutic benefits, as do dogs as companions. You will ultimately see that your healing is in your own hands. They will give you tools, strategies, and even medication for living with post-traumatic stress, but it is you who has the responsibility to practice the skills they give you to deal with it. You will probably not wake up some morning cured of PTSD, any more than muscle damage from a wound to your leg completely goes away. There is healing, but no cure. You owe it to yourself and to those who love you to struggle with post-traumatic stress, to understand what it is you have, what sets it off, and how to handle it. Healthy eating and exercise are of great benefit to veterans. This struggle may well be the most important you ever undertake, for yourself and for those who love you.

Take part in the group therapy the VA offers. It is important that we not isolate ourselves. Our veteran brothers and sisters care as much for our welfare as the VA professionals who help us. Vet Center-sponsored groups often become breakfast or lunch groups, sometimes with picnics and other activities that include families.

Concurrently with seeking treatment for PTSD (as well as TBI and other injuries or illnesses), file a claim with a local veterans services representative through your state's VA Regional Office. Our Congress voted to provide these benefits for you. You deserve the compensation money, special benefits, and priority access to VA medical care that come with a successful VA claim.

The VA is an imperfect human institution, with inconsistencies and imperfections. You have the right to seek another counselor or doctor if you have a personality or other conflict with the one you have. You have the right to question your doctor if you believe the medication prescribed is not working to your advantage. You have the right to appeal any VA decision with which you disagree, but seek the advice and help of your local veterans' services agencies before you file an appeal. We have the right to call attention to slow claims services and inadequate medical treatment when we find it, both for ourselves and for fellow veterans. That said, the less we come to think of the relationship between the VA and the veteran population as antagonistic, the better off we will all be. The neglect of the Vietnam veteran generation was the fault of Congress. These shortcomings were, at least in part, remedied by caring health professionals and by veterans working within the VA system.

The military services are also imperfect institutions, sometimes meting out draconian punishments in haste, sometimes failing to make perpetrators of assaults accountable for their actions. The military is but a reflection of the rest of our society. They are not plaster saints or demons in uniform.

Every veteran knows he cannot change the world. I can ruminate on my own helplessness, which is a common symptom of PTS. But I can also work on myself, my own family, my child-raising practices, and my relationships with others in my community.

In "Citizen Soldier" I offer suggestions for getting your education, on finding employment and on financial management. I claim no expertise in these matters. In fact, I have made the same mistakes I warn my younger readers about.

In the case of veterans of Iraq and Afghanistan, you are a small minority of Americans who have been to war, have seen humankind at its worst, and have served with some of the best. You have seen good people and innocent people die, and you have been in grave danger yourself. You may carry the visible, as well as the invisible wounds of war. Your fellow Americans need to hear from you in matters of national importance. If your conscience calls upon you to speak out, discuss or to lead, do so with the confidence of a veteran, of one who has been there.

How many times, in the course of my treatment for post-traumatic stress have I been told to "visualize" something that pleases me, for which I am thankful, or a desired outcome I would like to see happen in my life? Those who teach us yoga, tai chi or other relaxation techniques ask us to visualize the earth's energy being drawn up through our feet and discharged through our hands, toxins (real and imagined) leaving our bodies, and each in the face of "winds blow, typhoons roar, worlds collide; I remain undisturbed." When I visualize being relaxed in a tai chi session, I do, in fact, become relaxed.

Then I realized that we who struggle with post-traumatic stress are the masters of negative visualization. The images of catastrophe, doom, danger and loss we insist on carrying around have little if any objective truth. Imagining toxins leaving my body seems a bit more constructive than my personal litanies of fears, distrust and discontents.

We have examined the possibility and necessity for thinking in a different way. Scientific studies seem to show that our brains are malleable enough for us to train our minds to think differently. Suppose we could put the same energy and effort into visualizing ourselves as productive people, giving of our talents and skills to do some good in the world? Suppose we imagine ourselves walking up to receive the college degree for which we worked so hard? Can we visualize ourselves as loving a wife or husband more than ourselves, as being worthy of their trust? Can we see ourselves as loving parents? Can we imagine ourselves recognizing what it is we are dealing with, figuring out what triggers our habit-pattern behaviors, and getting on with our healing? Can we visualize gaining control over this disturbed thinking so that it happens only rarely, and being able to deal with it when it does? Can we visualize helping our brothers and sisters with their healing, just as they help us with ours?

Imagine.

Visualize.

Believe.

About the Author

Douglas Nelson is a veteran of the Vietnam conflict. His B.A. in Anthropology and M.A. in Education were earned at the College of William and Mary in Virginia. His forty-year civil service career includes writing and editing for the US Department of Defense, work as a contact representative for the Department of Veterans Affairs, and as a county veterans services representative for the County of Santa Clara, CA. He continues to advocate for veterans in California, where he lives with his wife.

APPENDIX A

Resources

www.va.gov The US Department of Veterans Affairs directs you to benefit information, facility locations and hours, and VA Forms.

http://www.cc.gatech.edu/fac/Thomas.Pilsch/Vietnam.html An excellent compilation of links to sites you can use to prove service in Vietnam or to document combat actions.

www.virtualwall.org Find brothers and sisters who were killed in Vietnam here. Search by name or unit.

http://www.cnn.com/SPECIALS/war.casualties/ Find brothers and sisters lost in OIF/OEF here.

http://www.gibill.va.gov/ Look here for details about the post 9-11 GI Bill.

http://www.coffeestrong.org/ This veteran-operated and owned coffee shop in Seattle serves all veterans and active-duty people with claims work, counseling and other support.

www.vets4vets.us/ This is a nationwide support group with local chapters. Search this site for a chapter in your area.

http://store.usgs.gov/pass/access_pass_application.pdf Get your National Parks pass with your award letter granting you service connected disability compensation.

www.StepToHealing.org This site provides an anonymous on-line self- assessment. Although it is aimed at active duty people, it is also useful for any veteran. You can find where to get help.

http://maketheconnection.net Find other veterans' stories. Realize that you are not alone, and that you certainly are not crazy. Someday you might want to add your own story.

The following are veterans' service organizations. All have service offices, usually co-located with your state's VA Regional Office.

http://www.legion.org/veteransbenefits/departmentofficers American Legion

http://www.vfw.org/ Veterans of Foreign Wars

http://www.dav.org/veterans/VeteransAffairs.aspx

Disabled American Veterans

http://www.purpleheart.org/ Military Order of the Purple Heart

http://www.fra.org/ Fleet Reserve Association

APPENDIX B

Books that Have Helped Me

<u>An Operator's Manual for Combat PTSD, Essays for Coping</u> by Ashley B. Hart, II Ph.D. Writer's Showcase, presented by Writer's Digest, 2000.

Dr. Hart works with veterans who struggle with PTS. His essays can be repetitive, but I think one or more of them will be as helpful to you as they were to me.

<u>Achilles in Vietnam Combat Trauma and the Undoing of Character</u> by Jonathan Shay, M.D., Ph.D., Scribner, 2002.

The author is a psychiatrist who has worked extensively with Vietnam combat veterans. If, as he states, that PTSD is the undoing of character, then our healing work, both for ourselves and in helping others, should be directed at the rebuilding of character.

<u>My Stroke of Insight: A Brain Scientists' Personal Journey</u> by Jill Bolte-Taylor, Ph.D., Viking, 2006.

This brain scientist recovered from a devastating stroke. She offers amazing insights into "left-brain/right-brain" function that I find very relevant to people who struggle with post-traumatic stress.

<u>Anger—Wisdom for Cooling the Flames</u> by Thich Nhat Hanh, Riverhead Books, The Berkley Publishing Group, 2001.

This author is a widely-published Buddhist spiritual teacher. Buddhism relies more heavily on practice than doctrine. Like many of us, he suffered greatly from the Vietnam war. He offers very practical advice for making peace with those we hurt, for cultivating "mindfulness", and for being "in the moment" in the face of anger, anxiety and hurt. Any of his books is well worth reading.

<u>PTSD, in Words and Pictures</u> by Clyde R. Horn, Robertson Publishing, 2011.

This friend and colleague shows what is possible, using his photographic and writing skills as self-expression. His book is a fine example of doing well what you do as therapy for your struggle with PTS.

APPENDIX C

Sample VA Forms 21-0781
(stressor statement)

Each of these was submitted to the VA as evidence to prove stressful incidents or conditions. Each of these stressor statements led to a successful disability compensation claim for PTSD.

Names of veterans, and of wounded or deceased comrades have been deleted to protect their privacy.

NOTE: If you have one or more of the combat awards discussed in Chapter 8, VA Form 21-0781 is, for you, unnecessary. Your combat award alone proves you were in combat.

OMB Approved No. 2900-0659
Respondent Burden: 1 Hour 10 Minutes

Department of Veterans Affairs

STATEMENT IN SUPPORT OF CLAIM FOR SERVICE CONNECTION FOR POST-TRAUMATIC STRESS DISORDER (PTSD)

INSTRUCTIONS: List the stressful incident or incidents that occurred in service that you feel contributed to your current condition. For each incident, provide a description of what happened, the date, the geographic location, your unit assignment and dates of assignment, and the full names and unit assignments of servicepersons you know of who were killed or injured during the incident. Please provide dates within at least a 60-day range and do not use nicknames. It is important that you complete the form in detail and be as specific as you can so that research of military records can be thoroughly conducted. If you do not know the answer, write "unknown." If more space is needed, attach a separate sheet, indicating the item number to which the answers apply.

1. NAME OF VETERAN (First, Middle, Last)	2. VA FILE NO.

STRESSFUL INCIDENT NO. 1

3A. DATE INCIDENT OCCURRED (Mo., day, yr.)	3B. LOCATION OF INCIDENT (City, State, Country, Province, landmark or military installation)
July 18, 2006	Fallujah, Iraq

3C. UNIT ASSIGNMENT DURING INCIDENT (Such as, DIVISION, WING, BATTALION, CAVALRY, SHIP)	3D. DATES OF UNIT ASSIGNMENT (Mo., day, yr.)	
	FROM	TO
Truck Company, HQ Battalion, 1st MARDIV	01/22/2006	02/07/2007

3E. DESCRIPTION OF THE INCIDENT

I was trained as a military vehicle driver. In Iraq I drove all sizes of cargo trucks, and HMMWV's, carrying all types of cargo and personnel. I also served as gunner on convoys. I did vehicle patrols and foot patrols. In Iraq, we are utilized as needed; we don't necessarily do exclusively what we were trained for.

While driving the lead truck in a convoy, I saw suspicious objects in the roadway. I followed procedure and drove through the "kill zone" and blocked the way with my truck, informing the rest of the convoy I saw a problem. The enemy did not usually target the first truck, which may have saved my life. The suspicious "trash" in the road turned out to be a concealed IED (improvised explosive device). The IED was disposed of, but I always wondered whether I would be in a similarly responsible situation and miss an IED, causing my buddies to be killed or wounded.

Every time we went out, we were subject to attack. People in my unit were wounded, and we knew soldiers and Marines were being killed in just such attacks every day in our area.

In an earlier incident, I believe April 2006 a buddy of mine was wounded in a truck behind me. I was in the lead vehicle and I wonder whether there was something in the road, wires or suspicious objects I should have seen.

3F. MEDALS OR CITATIONS YOU RECEIVED BECAUSE OF THE INCIDENT
Navy - Marine Corps Achievement Medal. See attached USMC narrative and citation for this award.

INFORMATION ABOUT SERVICEPERSONS WHO WERE KILLED OR INJURED DURING INCIDENT NO. 1
(ATTACH A SEPARATE SHEET IF MORE SPACE IS NEEDED)

4A. NAME OF SERVICEPERSON (First, Middle, Last)	4B. RANK	4C. DATE OF INJURY/DEATH (Mo., day, yr.)
Billy Ray Ricketts, III	LCPL	04/2006

4D. PLEASE CHECK ONE	4E. UNIT ASSIGNMENT DURING INCIDENT (Such as, DIVISION, WING, BATTALION, CAVALRY, SHIP)
☐ KILLED IN ACTION ☑ WOUNDED IN ACTION ☐ KILLED NON-BATTLE ☐ INJURED NON-BATTLE	Truck Company, HQ Battalion, 1st MARDIV

5A. NAME OF SERVICEPERSON (First, Middle, Last)	5B. RANK	5C. DATE OF INJURY/DEATH (Mo., day, yr.)

5D. PLEASE CHECK ONE	5E. UNIT ASSIGNMENT DURING INCIDENT (Such as, DIVISION, WING, BATTALION, CAVALRY, SHIP)
☐ KILLED IN ACTION ☐ WOUNDED IN ACTION ☐ KILLED NON-BATTLE ☐ INJURED NON-BATTLE	

VA FORM **21-0781**
JUL 2004

OMB Approved No. 2900-0659
Respondent Burden: 1 Hour 10 Minutes

	VA DATE STAMP
VA Department of Veterans Affairs	DO NOT WRITE IN THIS SPACE

STATEMENT IN SUPPORT OF CLAIM FOR SERVICE CONNECTION FOR POST-TRAUMATIC STRESS DISORDER (PTSD)

INSTRUCTIONS: List the stressful incident or incidents that occurred in service that you feel contributed to your current condition. For each incident, provide a description of what happened, the date, the geographic location, your unit assignment and dates of assignment, and the full names and unit assignments of servicepersons you know of who were killed or injured during the incident. Please provide dates within at least a 60-day range and do not use nicknames. It is important that you complete the form in detail and be as specific as you can so that research of military records can be thoroughly conducted. If you do not know the answer, write "unknown." If more space is needed, attach a separate sheet, indicating the item number to which the answers apply.

1. NAME OF VETERAN (First, Middle, Last)	2. VA FILE NO.

STRESSFUL INCIDENT NO. 1

3A. DATE INCIDENT OCCURRED (Mo., day, yr.)	3B. LOCATION OF INCIDENT (City, State, Country, Province, landmark or military installation)
01/2005	Tikrit, Iraq

3C. UNIT ASSIGNMENT DURING INCIDENT (Such as, DIVISION, WING, BATTALION, CAVALRY, SHIP)	3D. DATES OF UNIT ASSIGNMENT (Mo., day, yr.)	
	FROM	TO
467th Combat Engineer Company, 244th Engineer Battalion	12/18/2004	12/31/2005

3E. DESCRIPTION OF THE INCIDENT

One of my jobs as a combat engineer as as a "bomb hunter". This meant searching buildings along the way, when possible, as well as the road and surrounding structures.

A squad of us approached a damaged home and kicked open the door. Immediately we saw two adults dead, eyes open. Also we saw several dead small children. A boy of about 4 or 5 had been partially ripped open by some explosion.

I am of Middle Eastern origin. These children looked like my own. I cannot forget the shape they were in. I cannot forget the smell of the decaying bodies.

3F. MEDALS OR CITATIONS YOU RECEIVED BECAUSE OF THE INCIDENT

INFORMATION ABOUT SERVICEPERSONS WHO WERE KILLED OR INJURED DURING INCIDENT NO. 1
(ATTACH A SEPARATE SHEET IF MORE SPACE IS NEEDED)

4A. NAME OF SERVICEPERSON (First, Middle, Last)	4B. RANK	4C. DATE OF INJURY/DEATH (Mo., day, yr.)

4D. PLEASE CHECK ONE	4E. UNIT ASSIGNMENT DURING INCIDENT (Such as, DIVISION, WING, BATTALION, CAVALRY, SHIP)
☐ KILLED IN ACTION ☐ WOUNDED IN ACTION ☐ KILLED NON-BATTLE ☐ INJURED NON-BATTLE	

5A. NAME OF SERVICEPERSON (First, Middle, Last)	5B. RANK	5C. DATE OF INJURY/DEATH (Mo., day, yr.)

5D. PLEASE CHECK ONE	5E. UNIT ASSIGNMENT DURING INCIDENT (Such as, DIVISION, WING, BATTALION, CAVALRY, SHIP)
☐ KILLED IN ACTION ☐ WOUNDED IN ACTION ☐ KILLED NON-BATTLE ☐ INJURED NON-BATTLE	

VA FORM 21-0781
JUL 2004

VA Department of Veterans Affairs

STATEMENT IN SUPPORT OF CLAIM FOR SERVICE CONNECTION FOR POST-TRAUMATIC STRESS DISORDER (PTSD)

INSTRUCTIONS: List the stressful incident or incidents that occurred in service that you feel contributed to your current condition. For each incident, provide a description of what happened, the date, the geographic location, your unit assignment and dates of assignment, and the full names and unit assignments of servicepersons you know of who were killed or injured during the incident. Please provide dates within at least a 60-day range and do not use nicknames. It is important that you complete the form in detail and be as specific as you can so that research of military records can be thoroughly conducted. If you do not know the answer, write "unknown." If more space is needed, attach a separate sheet, indicating the item number to which the answers apply.

1. NAME OF VETERAN *(First, Middle, Last)*	2. VA FILE NO.

STRESSFUL INCIDENT NO. 1

3A. DATE INCIDENT OCCURRED *(Mo., day, yr.)*	3B. LOCATION OF INCIDENT *(City, State, Country, Province, landmark or military installation)*
13 November 1995	Riyadh Office of the Program Manager, Riyadh, Saudi Arabia

3C. UNIT ASSIGNMENT DURING INCIDENT *(Such as, DIVISION, WING, BATTALION, CAVALRY, SHIP)*	3D. DATES OF UNIT ASSIGNMENT *(Mo., day, yr.)*	
	FROM	TO
4409th Security Police Sqdn (local)..... home unit 100th Security Police Sqdn	12/1994	09/1997

3E. DESCRIPTION OF THE INCIDENT

Terrorists detonated a truck bomb at the Khobar Towers billets housing American service people in Riyadh, Saudi Arabia, killing 19. My unit , 100th SPS, was immediately tasked to deploy physical security by augmenting the on-site 4409th SPS. I was selected to deploy in direct and immediate response to this terrorist bombing and provide physical security of the premises during emergency personnel cleanup and recovery phase. By the time I arrived, only a few remained to be brought out, but the cleanup and recovery of remains lasted for months afterward.

3F. MEDALS OR CITATIONS YOU RECEIVED BECAUSE OF THE INCIDENT

Air Force Achievement Medal for Meritorious Service

INFORMATION ABOUT SERVICEPERSONS WHO WERE KILLED OR INJURED DURING INCIDENT NO. 1
(ATTACH A SEPARATE SHEET IF MORE SPACE IS NEEDED)

4A. NAME OF SERVICEPERSON *(First, Middle, Last)*	4B. RANK	4C. DATE OF INJURY/DEATH *(Mo., day, yr.)*
nineteen American service people		

4D. PLEASE CHECK ONE	4E. UNIT ASSIGNMENT DURING INCIDENT *(Such as, DIVISION, WING, BATTALION, CAVALRY, SHIP)*
☑ KILLED IN ACTION ☐ WOUNDED IN ACTION ☐ KILLED NON-BATTLE ☐ INJURED NON-BATTLE	

5A. NAME OF SERVICEPERSON *(First, Middle, Last)*	5B. RANK	5C. DATE OF INJURY/DEATH *(Mo., day, yr.)*

5D. PLEASE CHECK ONE	5E. UNIT ASSIGNMENT DURING INCIDENT *(Such as, DIVISION, WING, BATTALION, CAVALRY, SHIP)*
☐ KILLED IN ACTION ☐ WOUNDED IN ACTION ☐ KILLED NON-BATTLE ☐ INJURED NON-BATTLE	

VA FORM **21-0781**
JUL 2004

VA Department of Veterans Affairs

STATEMENT IN SUPPORT OF CLAIM FOR SERVICE CONNECTION FOR POST-TRAUMATIC STRESS DISORDER (PTSD)

INSTRUCTIONS: List the stressful incident or incidents that occurred in service that you feel contributed to your current condition. For each incident, provide a description of what happened, the date, the geographic location, your unit assignment and dates of assignment, and the full names and unit assignments of servicepersons you know of who were killed or injured during the incident. Please provide dates within at least a 60-day range and do not use nicknames. It is important that you complete the form in detail and be as specific as you can so that research of military records can be thoroughly conducted. If you do not know the answer, write "unknown." If more space is needed, attach a separate sheet, indicating the item number to which the answers apply.

1. NAME OF VETERAN (First, Middle, Last)	2. VA FILE NO.

STRESSFUL INCIDENT NO. 1

3A. DATE INCIDENT OCCURRED (Mo., day, yr.)	3B. LOCATION OF INCIDENT (City, State, Country, Province, landmark or military installation)
1945	Leyte, Philippines

3C. UNIT ASSIGNMENT DURING INCIDENT (Such as, DIVISION, WING, BATTALION, CAVALRY, SHIP)	3D. DATES OF UNIT ASSIGNMENT (Mo., day, yr.)	
	FROM	TO
714th Medical Sanitary Company		01/25/1946

3E. DESCRIPTION OF THE INCIDENT

I was a Staff Sergeant, in charge of my kitchen staff of very green, very scared young soldiers. We came ashore in a second wave of service troops. We went by convoy to Manila.

While debarking at Leyte Gulf, we were bombed from high altitude by Japanese bombers, beginning at dusk. I ordered my men to dig individual foxholes. When the bombs fell, we felt the concussions and shrapnel from the bombs. I was, of course, concerned for my own safety, but also for the safety of these young men for whom I was responsible.

3F. MEDALS OR CITATIONS YOU RECEIVED BECAUSE OF THE INCIDENT

INFORMATION ABOUT SERVICEPERSONS WHO WERE KILLED OR INJURED DURING INCIDENT NO. 1
(ATTACH A SEPARATE SHEET IF MORE SPACE IS NEEDED)

4A. NAME OF SERVICEPERSON (First, Middle, Last)	4B. RANK	4C. DATE OF INJURY/DEATH (Mo., day, yr.)

4D. PLEASE CHECK ONE	4E. UNIT ASSIGNMENT DURING INCIDENT (Such as, DIVISION, WING, BATTALION, CAVALRY, SHIP)
☐ KILLED IN ACTION ☐ WOUNDED IN ACTION ☐ KILLED NON-BATTLE ☐ INJURED NON-BATTLE	

5A. NAME OF SERVICEPERSON (First, Middle, Last)	5B. RANK	5C. DATE OF INJURY/DEATH (Mo., day, yr.)

5D. PLEASE CHECK ONE	5E. UNIT ASSIGNMENT DURING INCIDENT (Such as, DIVISION, WING, BATTALION, CAVALRY, SHIP)
☐ KILLED IN ACTION ☐ WOUNDED IN ACTION ☐ KILLED NON-BATTLE ☐ INJURED NON-BATTLE	

VA FORM 21-0781

	VA DATE STAMP DO NOT WRITE IN THIS SPACE

STATEMENT IN SUPPORT OF CLAIM FOR SERVICE CONNECTION FOR
POST-TRAUMATIC STRESS DISORDER (PTSD)

INSTRUCTIONS: List the stressful incident or incidents that occurred in service that you feel contributed to your current condition. For each incident, provide a description of what happened, the date, the geographic location, your unit assignment and dates of assignment, and the full names and unit assignments of servicepersons you know of who were killed or injured during the incident. Please provide dates within at least a 60-day range and do not use nicknames. It is important that you complete the form in detail and be as specific as you can so that research of military records can be thoroughly conducted. If you do not know the answer, write "unknown." If more space is needed, attach a separate sheet, indicating the item number to which the answers apply.

1. NAME OF VETERAN (First, Middle, Last)	2. VA FILE NO.

STRESSFUL INCIDENT NO. 1

3A. DATE INCIDENT OCCURRED (Mo., day, yr.)	3B. LOCATION OF INCIDENT (City, State, Country, Province, landmark or military installation)
March 13, 1968, late Tet Offensive	Camp Evans, I Corps Tactical Zone, RVN

3C. UNIT ASSIGNMENT DURING INCIDENT (Such as, DIVISION, WING, BATTALION, CAVALRY, SHIP)	3D. DATES OF UNIT ASSIGNMENT (Mo., day, yr.)	
	FROM	TO
371st Radio Research Company, in support of 1st Air Cavalry Div. (Airmobile)	01/1968	01/1969

3E. DESCRIPTION OF THE INCIDENT

My unit listened to enemy communications, and relayed radio direction finding locations from aircraft to division intelligence. We needed an antenna array to do our job. These antennas, I suppose, made us look important to the enemy.

Shortly after I arrived in the unit, I was introduced to the company commander. At the time, he was shovelling dirt out of a large hole that was to be our sandbagged bunker. I was assigned to be the night time radio operator.

At night, I was at my radio in the operations tent, with several sergeants. We heard mortar rounds being "walked" in, each one landing closer to us. CPT Casey yelled for us all to get under cover. Just after we reached the safety of the bunker he helped us to build, a mortar round landed with a loud whumping crash just outside. CPT Casey was hit as he was putting on his boots.

I was told to go out, with mortar rounds still impacting on Camp Evans, to look for an ambulance. I didn't know what an ambulance looked like, and came back without one. CPT Casey had already been taken away. I was yelled at for staring at pieces of him on the ground.

We didn't handle his loss very well. We never spoke of it among each other. I still don't handle it very well.

3F. MEDALS OR CITATIONS YOU RECEIVED BECAUSE OF THE INCIDENT

INFORMATION ABOUT SERVICEPERSONS WHO WERE KILLED OR INJURED DURING INCIDENT NO. 1
(ATTACH A SEPARATE SHEET IF MORE SPACE IS NEEDED)

4A. NAME OF SERVICEPERSON (First, Middle, Last)	4B. RANK	4C. DATE OF INJURY/DEATH (Mo., day, yr.)
John Michael Casey, Jr.	CPT	March 13, 1968

4D. PLEASE CHECK ONE	4E. UNIT ASSIGNMENT DURING INCIDENT (Such as, DIVISION, WING, BATTALION, CAVALRY, SHIP)
☑ KILLED IN ACTION ☐ WOUNDED IN ACTION ☐ KILLED NON-BATTLE ☐ INJURED NON-BATTLE	commanding officer, 371st Radio Research Company

5A. NAME OF SERVICEPERSON (First, Middle, Last)	5B. RANK	5C. DATE OF INJURY/DEATH (Mo., day, yr.)

5D. PLEASE CHECK ONE	5E. UNIT ASSIGNMENT DURING INCIDENT (Such as, DIVISION, WING, BATTALION, CAVALRY, SHIP)
☐ KILLED IN ACTION ☐ WOUNDED IN ACTION ☐ KILLED NON-BATTLE ☐ INJURED NON-BATTLE	

VA FORM **21-0781**
JUL 2004

VA DATE STAMP
DO NOT WRITE IN THIS SPACE

VA Department of Veterans Affairs

STATEMENT IN SUPPORT OF CLAIM FOR SERVICE CONNECTION FOR
POST-TRAUMATIC STRESS DISORDER (PTSD)

INSTRUCTIONS: List the stressful incident or incidents that occurred in service that you feel contributed to your current condition. For each incident, provide a description of what happened, the date, the geographic location, your unit assignment and dates of assignment, and the full names and unit assignments of servicepersons you know of who were killed or injured during the incident. Please provide dates within at least a 60-day range and do not use nicknames. It is important that you complete the form in detail and be as specific as you can so that research of military records can be thoroughly conducted. If you do not know the answer, write "unknown." If more space is needed, attach a separate sheet, indicating the item number to which the answers apply.

1. NAME OF VETERAN (First, Middle, Last)	2. VA FILE NO.

STRESSFUL INCIDENT NO. 1

3A. DATE INCIDENT OCCURRED (Mo., day, yr.)	3B. LOCATION OF INCIDENT (City, State, Country, Province, landmark or military installation)
	northern I Corps Tactical Zone, Camp Carroll, surrounding Landing Zones

3C. UNIT ASSIGNMENT DURING INCIDENT (Such as, DIVISION, WING, BATTALION, CAVALRY, SHIP)	3D. DATES OF UNIT ASSIGNMENT (Mo., day, yr.)	
	FROM	TO
A Battery, 1st Battalion ,12th Marine Artillery Regiment, 3rd Marine Division	12/1967	01/1968

3E. DESCRIPTION OF THE INCIDENT

I was trained as an artillery crewman on a 105mm howitzer. Being a fairly small howitzer, they and our ammunition were easily sling loaded by helicopter and placed on remote fire bases. We provided fire support where needed in the mountainous region just below the Demilitarized Zone.

Typically, we would have to build our own fire base after being dropped off with our guns. We immediately began digging our emplacements and filling sandbags. We were a small artillery battery of six (or fewer) guns, out there all by ourselves. When the enemy knew of our presence, we would get incoming mortar, rocket and even long range artillery fire. We were supplied by helicopter, but only in the morning, as they could not fly any other time. At nearly every firebase we could see the wreckage of helicopters that were shot down resupplying us. At times, they were shot down by enemy heavy machine gun fire as they were bringing us food, ammunition and mail. The helicopters were our only link with the outside; they brought new people in and took other Marines out, as well as the wounded and dead.

We were never safe on the ground depending on our own resources, or flying in or out of a firebase. We feared we would be told we were leaving for yet another firebase, another unknown situation. The stress of fearing for my life constantly, and of my underwear and socks rotting until I had none, and of being under constant fire wears on me to this day.

3F. MEDALS OR CITATIONS YOU RECEIVED BECAUSE OF THE INCIDENT

INFORMATION ABOUT SERVICEPERSONS WHO WERE KILLED OR INJURED DURING INCIDENT NO. 1
(ATTACH A SEPARATE SHEET IF MORE SPACE IS NEEDED)

4A. NAME OF SERVICEPERSON (First, Middle, Last)	4B. RANK	4C. DATE OF INJURY/DEATH (Mo., day, yr.)

4D. PLEASE CHECK ONE	4E. UNIT ASSIGNMENT DURING INCIDENT (Such as, DIVISION, WING, BATTALION, CAVALRY, SHIP)
☐ KILLED IN ACTION ☐ WOUNDED IN ACTION ☐ KILLED NON-BATTLE ☐ INJURED NON-BATTLE	

5A. NAME OF SERVICEPERSON (First, Middle, Last)	5B. RANK	5C. DATE OF INJURY/DEATH (Mo., day, yr.)

5D. PLEASE CHECK ONE	5E. UNIT ASSIGNMENT DURING INCIDENT (Such as, DIVISION, WING, BATTALION, CAVALRY, SHIP)
☐ KILLED IN ACTION ☐ WOUNDED IN ACTION ☐ KILLED NON-BATTLE ☐ INJURED NON-BATTLE	

VA FORM **21-0781**

VA Department of Veterans Affairs

STATEMENT IN SUPPORT OF CLAIM FOR SERVICE CONNECTION FOR POST-TRAUMATIC STRESS DISORDER (PTSD)

INSTRUCTIONS: List the stressful incident or incidents that occurred in service that you feel contributed to your current condition. For each incident, provide a description of what happened, the date, the geographic location, your unit assignment and dates of assignment, and the full names and unit assignments of servicepersons you know of who were killed or injured during the incident. Please provide dates within at least a 60-day range and do not use nicknames. It is important that you complete the form in detail and be as specific as you can so that research of military records can be thoroughly conducted. If you do not know the answer, write "unknown." If more space is needed, attach a separate sheet, indicating the item number to which the answers apply.

1. NAME OF VETERAN *(First, Middle, Last)*	2. VA FILE NO.

STRESSFUL INCIDENT NO. 1

3A. DATE INCIDENT OCCURRED *(Mo., day, yr.)*	3B. LOCATION OF INCIDENT *(City, State, Country, Province, landmark or military installation)*
	Da Nang, Dong Ha, Phu Bai I Corps Tactical Zone, RVN

3C. UNIT ASSIGNMENT DURING INCIDENT (Such as, DIVISION, WING, BATTALION, CAVALRY, SHIP)	3D. DATES OF UNIT ASSIGNMENT *(Mo., day, yr.)*	
	FROM	TO
Marine Air Support Sqdn 2, 1st Marine Air Wing	01/1966	01/1967

3E. DESCRIPTION OF THE INCIDENT

I was trained in ground communications and radar. I worked in tactical air control in Vietnam, communicating with aircraft. At Da Nang we were on the high ground, near the 1st Marine Division Headquarters. We took mortar and rocket fire because of our location.

At Dong Ha, near the DMZ, we took long range artillery fire, especially when supply aircraft came in. They could not land to unload, but, instead, put a parachute out the back to pull the load out so they could gain altitude again and get out. In those days, the battle for the DMZ that was to become the siege of Khe Sanh was raging. We were in the middle of it. Most of the time we lived behind sandbag walls. I feared for my life. I wondered when a chance shot would hit us directly. I never slept well the whole time I was in country. Next to us was a medical detachment (Charlie Med). Many mornings there would be rows of bodies in body bags outside the treatment tents. They were from Marines in the Dong Ha area, the unlucky. I always had the thought that I could be among them.

3F. MEDALS OR CITATIONS YOU RECEIVED BECAUSE OF THE INCIDENT

INFORMATION ABOUT SERVICEPERSONS WHO WERE KILLED OR INJURED DURING INCIDENT NO. 1
(ATTACH A SEPARATE SHEET IF MORE SPACE IS NEEDED)

4A. NAME OF SERVICEPERSON (First, Middle, Last)	4B. RANK	4C. DATE OF INJURY/DEATH *(Mo., day, yr.)*

4D. PLEASE CHECK ONE	4E. UNIT ASSIGNMENT DURING INCIDENT (Such as, DIVISION, WING, BATTALION, CAVALRY, SHIP)
☐ KILLED IN ACTION ☐ WOUNDED IN ACTION ☐ KILLED NON-BATTLE ☐ INJURED NON-BATTLE	

5A. NAME OF SERVICEPERSON *(First, Middle, Last)*	5B. RANK	5C. DATE OF INJURY/DEATH *(Mo., day, yr.)*

5D. PLEASE CHECK ONE	5E. UNIT ASSIGNMENT DURING INCIDENT (Such as, DIVISION, WING, BATTALION, CAVALRY, SHIP)
☐ KILLED IN ACTION ☐ WOUNDED IN ACTION ☐ KILLED NON-BATTLE ☐ INJURED NON-BATTLE	

VA FORM **21-0781**
JUL 2004

VA Department of Veterans Affairs

STATEMENT IN SUPPORT OF CLAIM FOR SERVICE CONNECTION FOR POST-TRAUMATIC STRESS DISORDER (PTSD)

INSTRUCTIONS: List the stressful incident or incidents that occurred in service that you feel contributed to your current condition. For each incident, provide a description of what happened, the date, the geographic location, your unit assignment and dates of assignment, and the full names and unit assignments of servicepersons you know of who were killed or injured during the incident. Please provide dates within at least a 60-day range and do not use nicknames. It is important that you complete the form in detail and be as specific as you can so that research of military records can be thoroughly conducted. If you do not know the answer, write "unknown." If more space is needed, attach a separate sheet, indicating the item number to which the answers apply.

1. NAME OF VETERAN (First, Middle, Last)	2. VA FILE NO.

STRESSFUL INCIDENT NO. 1

3A. DATE INCIDENT OCCURRED (Mo., day, yr.)	3B. LOCATION OF INCIDENT (City, State, Country, Province, landmark or military installation)
	based at Long Binh, III Corps Tactical Zone, flew missions all over Vietnam

3C. UNIT ASSIGNMENT DURING INCIDENT (Such as, DIVISION, WING, BATTALION, CAVALRY, SHIP)	3D. DATES OF UNIT ASSIGNMENT (Mo., day, yr.)	
	FROM	TO
9th Medical Laboratory	04/1971	04/1972

3E. DESCRIPTION OF THE INCIDENT

I was trained as a clerk-typist, and served in Vietnam with the 9th Medical Laboratory. We were an inter-service organization tasked with analyzing and treating the growing heroin problem at that time, by doing urine tests in various locations. We were based at Long Binh, but were flown by helicopter all over the country.

From our numerous flights on Huey helicopters, we took ground fire and returned fire, with our M16's and with the on-board M60 machine guns. I saw helicopters go down after being hit by ground fire. I saw wounded, dead and prisoners-of-war being brought in. Although we tried to numb ourselves to the stress of constant danger, by drinking or smoking marijuana, I feared for my life every time we went up. So many choppers were going down, and so many were being brought back dead and wounded that I thought it was inevitable that I would be next.

3F. MEDALS OR CITATIONS YOU RECEIVED BECAUSE OF THE INCIDENT

INFORMATION ABOUT SERVICEPERSONS WHO WERE KILLED OR INJURED DURING INCIDENT NO. 1
(ATTACH A SEPARATE SHEET IF MORE SPACE IS NEEDED)

4A. NAME OF SERVICEPERSON (First, Middle, Last)	4B. RANK	4C. DATE OF INJURY/DEATH (Mo., day, yr.)

4D. PLEASE CHECK ONE	4E. UNIT ASSIGNMENT DURING INCIDENT (Such as, DIVISION, WING, BATTALION, CAVALRY, SHIP)
☐ KILLED IN ACTION ☐ WOUNDED IN ACTION ☐ KILLED NON-BATTLE ☐ INJURED NON-BATTLE	

5A. NAME OF SERVICEPERSON (First, Middle, Last)	5B. RANK	5C. DATE OF INJURY/DEATH (Mo., day, yr.)

5D. PLEASE CHECK ONE	5E. UNIT ASSIGNMENT DURING INCIDENT (Such as, DIVISION, WING, BATTALION, CAVALRY, SHIP)
☐ KILLED IN ACTION ☐ WOUNDED IN ACTION ☐ KILLED NON-BATTLE ☐ INJURED NON-BATTLE	

VA FORM **21-0781**
JUL 2004

139

Department of Veterans Affairs

STATEMENT IN SUPPORT OF CLAIM FOR SERVICE CONNECTION FOR POST-TRAUMATIC STRESS DISORDER (PTSD)

INSTRUCTIONS: List the stressful incident or incidents that occurred in service that you feel contributed to your current condition. For each incident, provide a description of what happened, the date, the geographic location, your unit assignment and dates of assignment, and the full names and unit assignments of servicepersons you know of who were killed or injured during the incident. Please provide dates within at least a 60-day range and do not use nicknames. It is important that you complete the form in detail and be as specific as you can so that research of military records can be thoroughly conducted. If you do not know the answer, write "unknown." If more space is needed, attach a separate sheet, indicating the item number to which the answers apply.

1. NAME OF VETERAN *(First, Middle, Last)*	2. VA FILE NO.

STRESSFUL INCIDENT NO. 1

3A. DATE INCIDENT OCCURRED *(Mo., day, yr.)*	3B. LOCATION OF INCIDENT *(City, State, Country, Province, landmark or military installation)*
	Central Highlands, II Corps Tactical Zone, area around Pleiku

3C. UNIT ASSIGNMENT DURING INCIDENT (Such as, DIVISION, WING, BATTALION, CAVALRY, SHIP)	3D. DATES OF UNIT ASSIGNMENT *(Mo., day, yr.)*	
	FROM	TO
A Co., 2nd Battalion, 3rd Brigade, 25th Infantry Division	01/1967	09/1967

3E. DESCRIPTION OF THE INCIDENT

I was the company commander's radio operator in an infantry company. I was trained as a radio operator, but never used Morse Code.

We were in the bush nearly the whole time I was there. We stayed out for weeks at a time. Combat incidents were so frequent that I cannot isolate a particular one. I saw so many killed and wounded that I thought it was inevitable that I would be also. I was told I was a prime target, carrying the radio with its antenna. The man beside me was also a prime target, because the enemy presumed him to be an officer. A lieutenant beside me was killed. I did not get close to anyone because so many were lost or medevaced out. Several stepped onto mines or booby traps.

We laid ambushes and were ambushed by the enemy, both usually at night. I thought I had made it through this all right, but began to have emotional and other issues just as I got back .

3F. MEDALS OR CITATIONS YOU RECEIVED BECAUSE OF THE INCIDENT
I did not receive combat infantryman Badge because I did not have the infantry MOS.

INFORMATION ABOUT SERVICEPERSONS WHO WERE KILLED OR INJURED DURING INCIDENT NO. 1
(ATTACH A SEPARATE SHEET IF MORE SPACE IS NEEDED)

4A. NAME OF SERVICEPERSON (First, Middle, Last)	4B. RANK	4C. DATE OF INJURY/DEATH *(Mo., day, yr.)*

4D. PLEASE CHECK ONE	4E. UNIT ASSIGNMENT DURING INCIDENT (Such as, DIVISION, WING, BATTALION, CAVALRY, SHIP)
☐ KILLED IN ACTION ☐ WOUNDED IN ACTION ☐ KILLED NON-BATTLE ☐ INJURED NON-BATTLE	

5A. NAME OF SERVICEPERSON *(First, Middle, Last)*	5B. RANK	5C. DATE OF INJURY/DEATH *(Mo., day, yr.)*

5D. PLEASE CHECK ONE	5E. UNIT ASSIGNMENT DURING INCIDENT (Such as, DIVISION, WING, BATTALION, CAVALRY, SHIP)
☐ KILLED IN ACTION ☐ WOUNDED IN ACTION ☐ KILLED NON-BATTLE ☐ INJURED NON-BATTLE	

VA FORM **21-0781**
JUL 2004

140

VA Department of Veterans Affairs

STATEMENT IN SUPPORT OF CLAIM FOR SERVICE CONNECTION FOR POST-TRAUMATIC STRESS DISORDER (PTSD)

INSTRUCTIONS: List the stressful incident or incidents that occurred in service that you feel contributed to your current condition. For each incident, provide a description of what happened, the date, the geographic location, your unit assignment and dates of assignment, and the full names and unit assignments of servicepersons you know of who were killed or injured during the incident. Please provide dates within at least a 60-day range and do not use nicknames. It is important that you complete the form in detail and be as specific as you can so that research of military records can be thoroughly conducted. If you do not know the answer, write "unknown." If more space is needed, attach a separate sheet, indicating the item number to which the answers apply.

1. NAME OF VETERAN *(First, Middle, Last)*	2. VA FILE NO.

STRESSFUL INCIDENT NO. 1

3A. DATE INCIDENT OCCURRED *(Mo., day, yr.)*	3B. LOCATION OF INCIDENT *(City, State, Country, Province, landmark or military installation)*
	area of Camp Slayer, Iraq

3C. UNIT ASSIGNMENT DURING INCIDENT *(Such as, DIVISION, WING, BATTALION, CAVALRY, SHIP)*	3D. DATES OF UNIT ASSIGNMENT *(Mo., day, yr.)*	
	FROM	TO
322nd Civil Affairs Brigade	06/2005	07/2006

3E. DESCRIPTION OF THE INCIDENT

I had supply and infantry experience, and these skills were utilized by my civil affairs unit. I handled supplies, delivered them, drove civil affairs personnel to assignments, and any tasks needed by my unit. During the day we were out in the villages, advising, supervising self-help projects, and facilitating communication between us and the local people.

On our convoys out and back to Camp Slayer, we came under sniper fire and sometimes took IED attacks. We were not combat troops, or ambush reaction forces. The enemy knew we were civil affairs, and "soft" targets.

All too often we saw the dead from IED's and bombs, simply civilian women, kids, old men who happened to be in the way. There was no time for the local police to clean up the bodies, so we had to drive around them. I thought often that, if this happened to innocent people who were not the intended targets, then it could happen to me, much of the time an intended target.

3F. MEDALS OR CITATIONS YOU RECEIVED BECAUSE OF THE INCIDENT

INFORMATION ABOUT SERVICEPERSONS WHO WERE KILLED OR INJURED DURING INCIDENT NO. 1
(ATTACH A SEPARATE SHEET IF MORE SPACE IS NEEDED)

4A. NAME OF SERVICEPERSON *(First, Middle, Last)*	4B. RANK	4C. DATE OF INJURY/DEATH *(Mo., day, yr.)*

4D. PLEASE CHECK ONE	4E. UNIT ASSIGNMENT DURING INCIDENT *(Such as, DIVISION, WING, BATTALION, CAVALRY, SHIP)*
☐ KILLED IN ACTION ☐ WOUNDED IN ACTION ☐ KILLED NON-BATTLE ☐ INJURED NON-BATTLE	

5A. NAME OF SERVICEPERSON *(First, Middle, Last)*	5B. RANK	5C. DATE OF INJURY/DEATH *(Mo., day, yr.)*

5D. PLEASE CHECK ONE	5E. UNIT ASSIGNMENT DURING INCIDENT *(Such as, DIVISION, WING, BATTALION, CAVALRY, SHIP)*
☐ KILLED IN ACTION ☐ WOUNDED IN ACTION ☐ KILLED NON-BATTLE ☐ INJURED NON-BATTLE	

VA FORM **21-0781**
JUL 2004

VA Department of Veterans Affairs

STATEMENT IN SUPPORT OF CLAIM FOR SERVICE CONNECTION FOR POST-TRAUMATIC STRESS DISORDER (PTSD)

INSTRUCTIONS: List the stressful incident or incidents that occurred in service that you feel contributed to your current condition. For each incident, provide a description of what happened, the date, the geographic location, your unit assignment and dates of assignment, and the full names and unit assignments of servicepersons you know of who were killed or injured during the incident. Please provide dates within at least a 60-day range and do not use nicknames. It is important that you complete the form in detail and be as specific as you can so that research of military records can be thoroughly conducted. If you do not know the answer, write "unknown." If more space is needed, attach a separate sheet, indicating the item number to which the answers apply.

1. NAME OF VETERAN (First, Middle, Last)	2. VA FILE NO.

STRESSFUL INCIDENT NO. 1

3A. DATE INCIDENT OCCURRED (Mo., day, yr.)	3B. LOCATION OF INCIDENT (City, State, Country, Province, landmark or military installation)
1963-64, 1965	GULF OF TONKIN

3C. UNIT ASSIGNMENT DURING INCIDENT (Such as, DIVISION, WING, BATTALION, CAVALRY, SHIP)	3D. DATES OF UNIT ASSIGNMENT (Mo., day, yr.)	
	FROM	TO
USS EVERSOLE (DD-789)	1963	1964, also 1965

3E. DESCRIPTION OF THE INCIDENT

I was trained as a radar operator in the ship's combat information center. I had a Top Secret Crypto Security clearance. My ship provided fire support with our 5-inch guns and interdicted enemy resupply shipping (small sampan-like boats). Part of our mission was to operate north of Hainan Island to provide rescue capability in support of carrier operations.

We were tasked with following a Soviet nuclear submarine out of Haiphong harbor. We kept it in radar and in visual sight. That sub could have destroyed us. The, sub surfaced, the crew came up on deck, they waved, and dove out of sight. Part of the radar function was to keep the ship on course during fire support operations.
We could easily have been targeted by shore batteries or small arms. We picked up enemy aircraft on these northern missions. From the direction of flight, we believed them to be MIG aircraft out of China.
As a radarman, I was always aware of threats to our ship. I did not necessarily share this knowledge, but all knew of many threats, anyway. Many sightings were visual, as these aircraft overflew our ship. When this happened, we went to General Quarters status. My shipmates and I feared for our lives.

3F. MEDALS OR CITATIONS YOU RECEIVED BECAUSE OF THE INCIDENT

INFORMATION ABOUT SERVICEPERSONS WHO WERE KILLED OR INJURED DURING INCIDENT NO. 1
(ATTACH A SEPARATE SHEET IF MORE SPACE IS NEEDED)

4A. NAME OF SERVICEPERSON (First, Middle, Last)	4B. RANK	4C. DATE OF INJURY/DEATH (Mo., day, yr.)

4D. PLEASE CHECK ONE ☐ KILLED IN ACTION ☐ WOUNDED IN ACTION ☐ KILLED NON-BATTLE ☐ INJURED NON-BATTLE	4E. UNIT ASSIGNMENT DURING INCIDENT (Such as, DIVISION, WING, BATTALION, CAVALRY, SHIP)

5A. NAME OF SERVICEPERSON (First, Middle, Last)	5B. RANK	5C. DATE OF INJURY/DEATH (Mo., day, yr.)

5D. PLEASE CHECK ONE ☐ KILLED IN ACTION ☐ WOUNDED IN ACTION ☐ KILLED NON-BATTLE ☐ INJURED NON-BATTLE	5E. UNIT ASSIGNMENT DURING INCIDENT (Such as, DIVISION, WING, BATTALION, CAVALRY, SHIP)

VA FORM **21-0781**

OMB Control No. 2900-0659
Respondent Burden: 1 Hour 10 Minutes

Department of Veterans Affairs

VA DATE STAMP
DO NOT WRITE IN THIS SPACE

STATEMENT IN SUPPORT OF CLAIM FOR SERVICE CONNECTION FOR POST-TRAUMATIC STRESS DISORDER (PTSD)

INSTRUCTIONS: List the stressful incident or incidents that occurred in service that you feel contributed to your current condition. For each incident, provide a description of what happened, the date, the geographic location, your unit assignment and dates of assignment, and the full names and unit assignments of servicepersons you know of who were killed or injured during the incident. Please provide dates within at least a 60-day range and do not use nicknames. It is important that you complete the form in detail and be as specific as you can so that research of military records can be thoroughly conducted. If you do not know the answer, write "unknown." If more space is needed, attach a separate sheet, indicating the item number to which the answers apply.

1. NAME OF VETERAN (First, Middle, Last)	2. VA FILE NO.

STRESSFUL INCIDENT NO. 1

3A. DATE INCIDENT OCCURRED (Mo., day, yr.)	3B. LOCATION OF INCIDENT (City, State, Country, Province, landmark or military installation)
Dec 11, 1973	USS Kitty Hawk, Pacific cruise, '73

3C. UNIT ASSIGNMENT DURING INCIDENT (Such as, DIVISION, WING, BATTALION, CAVALRY, SHIP)	3D. DATES OF UNIT ASSIGNMENT (Mo., day, yr.)	
	FROM	TO
USS Kitty Hawk CVA-63	07-1973	5/26/1977

3E. DESCRIPTION OF THE INCIDENT

My job was fireman. We were sent down toward the engine room to fight a fire, but it was over before I got there.

I knew Kevin Johnson from Navy boot camp. He and I talked a lot, hung out together, and enjoyed going on liberty.

I learned the next day that Johnson was one of the five sailors who died in that fire. I knew he did engine room work, was one of the "bilge rats".

Burning to death was a horrible way for my friend to go. Out of 5000 sailors on that ship, my friend was one who had to die.

In my sleep I smell the smoke and scorched metal and paint and feel the heat.

3F. MEDALS OR CITATIONS YOU RECEIVED BECAUSE OF THE INCIDENT

INFORMATION ABOUT SERVICEPERSONS WHO WERE KILLED OR INJURED DURING INCIDENT NO. 1
(ATTACH A SEPARATE SHEET IF MORE SPACE IS NEEDED)

4A. NAME OF SERVICEPERSON (First, Middle, Last)	4B. RANK	4C. DATE OF INJURY/DEATH (Mo., day, yr.)
Kevin Johnson and four other sailors	FR	Dec 11, 1973

4D. PLEASE CHECK ONE	4E. UNIT ASSIGNMENT DURING INCIDENT (Such as, DIVISION, WING, BATTALION, CAVALRY, SHIP)
☐ KILLED IN ACTION ☐ WOUNDED IN ACTION ☑ KILLED NON-BATTLE ☐ INJURED NON-BATTLE	USS Kitty Hawk CVA-63

5A. NAME OF SERVICEPERSON (First, Middle, Last)	5B. RANK	5C. DATE OF INJURY/DEATH (Mo., day, yr.)
Many more sailors		

5D. PLEASE CHECK ONE	5E. UNIT ASSIGNMENT DURING INCIDENT (Such as, DIVISION, WING, BATTALION, CAVALRY, SHIP)
☐ KILLED IN ACTION ☑ WOUNDED IN ACTION ☐ KILLED NON-BATTLE ☑ INJURED NON-BATTLE	

VA FORM
JUL 2004 **21-0781**

143

APPENDIX D

Agent Orange

If you are a Viet Nam veteran who served "boots-on-the-ground" or in inland waterways in-country, you were exposed to a dioxin-based herbicide, Agent Orange. The VA may concede exposure for certain Korea and Thailand veterans. These herbicides were usually sprayed from aircraft or by ground dispersal. Agent Orange was used to defoliate jungle areas, but also to deny the enemy rice and agricultural products. By law, if we served in Vietnam, we were exposed. The law does not distinguish between work in an air-conditioned office at MACV Headquarters and being in the bush 365 days.

Our government poisoned us. It is that simple. If the corporations manufacturing these herbicides tested their effects on the human body, these tests did not figure into the military expediency of their widespread use. We were expendable. Our country acted with callous disregard for our health and the health of the

Vietnamese who still farm this land, drink its water, and eat its marine and aquatic life.

Each Vietnam vet should present his or her DD214 to the nearest VA medical facility and request the Agent Orange exam. You will be checked for the health issues on the list of Agent Orange disabilities. You will very likely be told you have none of them. Be happy, take your wife out to dinner. Have wine with dinner.

Should any of these disabilities on this list show up, get it treated by the VA at no cost to you, and get to a veterans services office to file your VA compensation claim. You can also do your own claim. If this is your first VA disability claim, fill out VA Form 21-526. Read the instructions on the form carefully. If this is a subsequent claim, do VA Form 526B. In either case, tell the VA who is treating your disability. The VA will request VA treatment records. If you are receiving private treatment, get the records from your doctor and submit them with your claim.

As a vet rep, the three most common Agent Orange disabilities I see are prostate cancer, diabetes mellitus Type II and its complications, and ischemic heart disease. Diabetes and ischemic heart disease are made worse by the pernicious junk the American food industry is pushing at us. High fructose corn syrup is insidious; it is found in such seemingly innocuous foods as ketchup, pickle relish, salad dressings, breakfast cereals and snack bars. The more processed a food is, the more likely it is to be high in unnecessary carbohydrates and salt.

As a Vietnam veteran with diabetes, I urge you to throw out over-processed boxed and canned junk. Eat lean meats, fish, chicken, vegetables, fruits and nuts and you will feel better. Purge the poisons of excess sugar and salt from your body. Part of my problem was overeating. Take the VA classes in diet and portion size. Walk at least 40 minutes a day. You will lose weight and look better, in addition to feeling better. If your doctor prescribes medication, take it with the thought of letting it help you while you need the help.

<u>List of Agent Orange Disabilities Recognized by the US Department of Veterans Affairs</u> (List adapted from that given on the VA web page)

1. <u>Diabetes Mellitus, Type II and Its Complications</u> Common complications, in addition to high blood sugar, are peripheral neuropathy in the feet and/or hands, diabetic retinopathy and impotence.

2. <u>Ischemic Heart Disease</u> is the accumulation of plaques in the aortic arteries. Do not confuse this with heart arrhythmia issues.

3. <u>Cancer of the Prostate</u> is often found as a result of a high blood PSA reading. A biopsy can confirm or rule out cancer.

4. Respiratory Cancers are in the lungs, larynx, trachea and bronchus.

5. Multiple Myeloma is a cancer of the white blood cells in bone marrow.

6. Parkinson's Disease is a progressive disorder of the nervous system.

7. Chronic B-Cell Leukemias are a type of cancer affecting white blood cells.

8. Soft Tissue Sarcoma (other than osteosarcoma, chondrosarcoma, Kaposi's sarcoma or mesothelioma) are cancers found in muscle, connective tissue fat, blood and lymph.

9. Porphyria Cutanea Tarda is characterized by liver dysfunction and by thinning and blistering of the skin in sun-exposed areas. It must have shown up within a year of exposure and must have been at least 10% disabling.

10. Hodgkin's Disease is a malignant lymphoma (cancer) that causes progressive enlargement of the lymph nodes, liver and spleen, and anemia.

11. Non-Hodgkins Lymphoma is a group of cancers affecting lymph nodes and other lymphatic tissue.

12. AL Amyloidosis is a rare disease caused by abnormal protein, amyloid, in organs and tissues.

13. <u>Acute and Sub-acute Peripheral Neuropathy</u>, when not associated with diabetes, must be at least 10% disabling and appear within a year of exposure to herbicides. Peripheral neuropathy in Vietnam veterans is most often associated with diabetes Mellitus Type II.

14. <u>Chloracne</u> is a skin condition that appears soon after exposure to certain chemicals, resembling common teenage acne. It must have shown up within a year of exposure and must have been at least 10% disabling.

Glossary

Note: If the acronym is in wider usage than the spelled-out term, the acronym will be given first.

<u>Agent Orange</u> is the term for the various dioxin-based herbicides used in Vietnam and in other areas. It was usually sprayed from aircraft, but was also ground-dispersed. Exposure is tied to several specific health problems.

<u>Board for the Correction of Military Records</u>, (BCMR) a board of three to five high-ranking civilian officers of each branch of military service meeting to decide discharge upgrade cases initiated by DD Form 149

<u>Captain</u> (CPT) an officer rank of varying pay grades according to the specific military service. An Army or Marine Corps captain commands a company.

<u>Compensation</u> is a monetary benefit paid to veterans for injury or illness caused or aggravated by military service.

<u>C&P (Compensation and Pension)</u> The VA Regional Office sends compensation and pension disability cases to doctors in the VA health care system for medical opinions. These appointments are called C&P exams.

<u>DD Forms</u> are used for US Department of Defense administrative matters.

<u>DD Form 149</u> Application for Correction of Military Records

<u>DD 214</u> the official record of discharge from military service.

<u>DD Form 293</u> Application for the Review of Discharge from the Armed Forces of the United States

<u>Discharge Review Board, (DRB)</u> five military officers from each branch of military service meeting to decide military discharge upgrade cases less than fifteen years old, or those initiated by DD Form 293.

<u>E4</u> is the fourth military enlisted pay grade. Most soldiers attain this rank during their first enlistment.

<u>Emotional Freedom Therapy (EFT)</u> is a therapy method involving identifying and accepting emotions.

<u>Eye Movement Desensitization and Reprocessing (EMDR)</u> is a therapy method dealing directly with

traumatic events, involving bodily and eye movement, and the emotions.

Forward Operating Base (FOB) a military installation in a hostile area offering supply, medical and combat support

HMMWV (pronounced "Humvee") High-Mobility, Multipurpose Wheeled Vehicle, a 1 ¼-ton truck used for cargo and personnel transport, the signature military vehicle of the US military in OIF/OEF

Huey a helicopter of the UH-1-series used for many transport purposes in Vietnam

IED (Improvised Explosive Device) explosive devices made from a variety of artillery projectiles or demolition charges, detonated by fuze, wire or remote means

Individual Unemployability (I/U) is a VA term for the 100% disability rate paid to a seriously disabled veteran because he is judged to be unable to obtain and hold gainful employment.

MACV (Military Assistance Command, Vietnam) the American military command structure, military headquarters

Medevac a military term for the evacuation of casualties to places of treatment

MOS military occupational specialty, one's military job

NCO (Non-Commissioned Officer) is an enlisted military person having first level or higher supervisory or leadership responsibility. A corporal and a sergeant major have specific levels of responsibility, but both are NCO's.

OIF/OEF (Operation Iraqi Freedom, Operation Enduring Freedom) This term is for the period of military service following the 09/11/2001 attacks. Its usage continues through the present time.

PCS, Permanent Change of Station a change in work location, mandated by official orders

Pension refers to the VA Disability Pension, for permanently and totally disabled wartime veterans who are needy, or to the Death Pension for needy spouses of deceased veterans.

Post-Traumatic Stress Disorder (PTSD) is the term used in the psychology profession's Diagnostic and Statistical Manual, Edition V for treatment purposes and by the U.S. Department of Veteran Affairs for purposes of describing specified behaviors and thought patterns as a service-connected disability. The term Post-Traumatic Stress (PTS) is receiving wider use in treatment circles as describing the conditions experienced by a patient who is actively involved in the treatment process.

ROTC (Reserve Officers Training Corps) college-level military training culminating in officer rank upon graduation.

<u>R&R (Rest and Relaxation)</u> was a five-day, or longer period of relief from military duties, often involving a trip to a resort area away from hostilities.

<u>TBI (Traumatic Brain Injury)</u> is any trauma to the brain, including open head injuries, projectile wounds, concussion injuries from external causes impacting normal brain function.

<u>VA (The United States Department of Veterans Affairs)</u> is the cabinet-level Federal Agency charged with running the veterans' health care system, administering compensation and pension benefits, GI Bill education benefits, and veterans' cemeteries. "VA" was the term used by veterans for the Veterans Administration, as it was formerly known.

<u>VCAA (Veterans Claims Assistance Act)</u> is a term rapidly falling into disuse. It refers to a remedial process brought on by a legal case in which a veteran successfully claimed he did not receive adequate notice before his case was decided. The VCAA letter is an invitation to the veteran to gather any remaining evidence he considers pertinent to his case.

<u>WWI</u> World War I

<u>WWII</u> World War II

CPSIA information can be obtained at www.ICGtesting.com
Printed in the USA
BVOW04s1541261113

337385BV00001B/2/P

9 781452 581316